Writing with Multiple Intelligences

Edna Kovacs, Ph.D.

Blue Heron Publishing § Portland, Oregon

Writing with Multiple Intelligences by Edna Kovacs, Ph.D.

Printed and bound in the United States of America.

This project was partially funded by a grant from the Portland-based Regional Arts & Culture Council.

Cover design: Sue Tencza
Book design: Dennis Stovall

Published by
Blue Heron Publishing
420 S.W. Washington Street
Suite 303
Portland, Oregon 97204
503.221.6841
info@blueheronpublishing.com
www.blueheronpublishing.com

ISBN 0-936085-43-6

PUBLISHERS'S CATALOGING-IN-PUBLICATION DATA

Kovacs, Edna.
    Writing with multiple intelligences

    p. : ill.; cm.
    ISBN: 0-936085-43-6

1. Creative writing — Studying and teaching. 2. Art therapy — Study and application. 3. Poetics —Studying and teaching. I.
TITLE

First edition.
10 9 8 7 6 5 4 3 2 1

Contents

Chapter Four

Acknowledgments

This book was made possible in part by a Literature Grant from the Regional Arts and Culture Council and Blue Heron Publishing. The author would like to thank Dennis Stovall, Publisher, and Martha Ruttle, Marketing Director, and Daniel Urban, Editorial Director, for helping me realize my artistic vision.

Grateful acknowledgment to Sheila Bender, Gail Brophy, Ph.D., Christine Caton, Geraldine DeLuca, Ph.D., and Carlos Reyes for their letters of support and encouragement; to the members of the Literary Arts panel and Director of Grants and Community Programs, Alberto Rafouls.

Thanks also to Lisa Barnes at the Regional Arts and Culture Council, David Hedges of the Oregon State Poetry Association, Christopher Zinn of the Oregon Council for the Humanities, and Laura Cohen and Jane Reid of Young Audiences, who kept my phone ringing with opportunities to teach writing in communities throughout Oregon.

Deep appreciation goes out to the members of my doctoral committee at the Union Institute Graduate School: Carol Barrett, Ph.D., Geraldine DeLuca, Ph.D., Ellie Friedland, Ph.D., Peggy Osna Heller, Ph.D., Susan Makin, Ph.D., and Roni Natov, Ph.D.; to the faculty whose experiential learning seminars gave me an abundance of material to draw from;

to the Center for Journal Therapy for the instruction and certification that helps guide me and others through our days; to Jonathan and Nancy Foust and the Kripalu Yoga Center; to the Oregon Council for the Humanities' Chautauqua in the Schools program; to David Hedges and the Family Poetry Workshop Project, a project of the Oregon State Poetry Association in partnership with the Center for the Book at the Oregon State Library, made possible by grants from the Oregon Community Foundation, the Collins Foundation, and contributions from community libraries; to the Regional Arts and Culture Council's Arts-in-Education and Neighborhood Arts Programs; to the Wordsworth Center for Poetry Therapy for their instruction and lifelong learning; and to Young Audiences of Oregon and Southwest Washington, Inc.

Many thanks to Nancy Nordhoff, Director, and the Hedgebrook Foundation on Whidbey Island, Washington, for the writing fellowship which gave this poet with a camera the opportunity to photograph some of the visuals that appear in this text.

And most of all, special thanks goes out to my family and friends who believed in me throughout this journey within a journey.

Introduction

How can I make the creative process accessible to people with different learning styles?

What creative techniques can I apply to my teaching?

How is the creative process a healing one?

How can writing encourage people to explore new ways of thinking and understanding?

These are the questions that *Writing with Multiple Intelligences* explores. Bring your pen and notebooks with you, for you will want to try many of these exercises yourself. I have been told that I have a gift for cultivating an appreciation for writing. This creative writing handbook is about returning that gift.

I have combined elements of the expressive arts, multicultural studies, education, and psychology in this book. Like David Lazear, and others who have constructed educational strategies based upon Howard Gardner's theory of multiple intelligences, I recognize eight styles of learning: body/kinesthetic, interpersonal, intrapersonal, logical/mathematical, musical/rhythmic, naturalist, verbal/linguistic, and visual/spatial. Conceptualizing the learning experience in terms of these eight categories helps me teach writing to students with varied interests, strengths, and learning styles.

The demarcation of learning styles suggests to me that creative learning is cyclic, which is why I have organized the contents of this book into four chapters that correspond to the cycle of seasons. Each chapter, with the exception of chapter 4, is subsequently divided into sections that correspond to specific intelligences or styles of learning. You will find that many of the exercises in these sections involve more than one of the multiple intelligences and that they are all intrapersonal, as this is the nature of writing. The fourth chapter focuses on intrapersonal intelligence itself. This book is, above all else, about writing from within.

Multiple Intelligences: Gardner and Lazear

Howard Gardner, originator of the multiple intelligences theory, writes in *The Creative Spirit*, "A person isn't creative in general—you can't just say a person is 'creative.' You have to say he or she is creative in X, whether it's writing, being a teacher, or running an organization. Creativity isn't some kind of fluid that can ooze in any direction. The life of the mind is divided into different regions which I call 'intelligences,' like math, language, or music."

Gardner's theory of multiple intelligences moves beyond Piaget's cognitive development theory, which focuses on the biological foundations of intelligence. Instead of studying its biological foundations, Gardner explores intelligence in terms of "frames of mind." David Lazear and others have incorporated the concept of multiple intelligences into more traditional curricula by constructing interdisciplinary educational strategies. Lazear's model of teaching for multiple intelligences was presented at a National Council for Teachers of English conference that I attended in Chicago in November 1996. As I reflected on the way this model honors all kinds of learners, I began to formulate and explore ways to teach writing through each of the intelligences.

Lazear's model defines the eight styles of learning as follows:

1. LINGUISTIC LEARNER
"The Word Player"
    LIKES TO read, write, tell stories
    LEARNS BEST BY saying, hearing, and seeing
      words

2. LOGICAL/MATHEMATICAL LEARNER
"The Questioner"
    LIKES TO do experiments, figure things out, work with
      numbers, ask questions, explore patterns and rela-
      tionships
    IS GOOD AT math, reasoning, logic, problem-solving
    LEARNS BEST BY categorizing, classifying, working
      with abstract patterns/relationships

3. SPATIAL LEARNER
"The Visualizer"
    LIKES TO draw, build, design and create things, day-
      dream, look at pictures/slides, watch movies, play
      with machines such as computers
    IS GOOD AT imagining things, sensing changes, com-
      pleting mazes/puzzles, reading maps and charts
    LEARNS BEST BY visualizing, dreaming, using the
      mind's eye, working with colors/pictures

4. MUSICAL LEARNER
"The Music Lover"

LIKES TO sing, hum tunes, listen to music, play an instrument, respond to music

IS GOOD AT picking up sounds, remembering melodies, noticing pitches/rhythms, keeping time

LEARNS BEST BY rhythm, melody, music

5. BODILY/KINESTHETIC LEARNER
"The Mover"

LIKES TO move around, touch and talk, use body language

IS GOOD AT physical activities (sports/dance/acting), crafts

LEARNS BEST BY touching, moving, interacting with space, processing knowledge through bodily sensations

6. INTERPERSONAL LEARNER
"The Socializer"

LIKES TO have lots of friends, talk to people, join groups

IS GOOD AT understanding people, leading others, organizing, communicating, manipulating, mediating conflicts

LEARNS BEST BY sharing, comparing, relating, cooperating, interviewing

7. INTRAPERSONAL LEARNER
"The Individual"

LIKES TO work alone, pursue own interests

IS GOOD AT understanding self, focusing inward on feelings/dreams, following instincts, pursuing interests/goals, being original

LEARNS BEST BY working alone, individualized projects, self-paced instruction, having own space

8. NATURALIST LEARNER
"At Home in Nature"

  LIKES TO explore the natural world, from the microscopic world to what can be perceived with the naked eye, the senses of taste, touch, smell, sound, and the inner senses of the human spirit (i.e., being "moved" and touched by nature)

  IS GOOD AT recognizing and classifying different species, exploring the five traditional senses, recognizing the effect of nature on the "inner world" of the self

  LEARNS BEST BY direct experience, working alone and with others

Writing with Multiple Intelligences: A Framework

Each chapter in this book offers exercises that use the senses to fuel creative expression through writing. All of the writing and teaching methods in this book focus on exploring, enhancing, and discovering the healing powers of creativity for personal as well as planetary growth.

Spring is a time for awakening and cultivating our minds, bodies, and spirits. We can be vibrant and notice all details—the outline of a leaf, the caw of a crow. We can laugh and sing like children. The first chapter, "Spring," is subtitled "Beginner's Mind: A Time for Budding." This chapter focuses on collaborative writing, writing from the body, and the naturalist intelligence.

Summer is a time for watching our gardens grow, listening to nature, and becoming attuned to the colors, textures, tempos, timbres, and pitches of the world around us. It is a time for celebrating the joy of being alive. I subtitled the second chapter "Blossoming." Photo writing and writing with music ideas abound in this chapter.

Autumn ripens our fruit, creating a harvest-time of abundance. We honor our relationships with others and with the world around us. It is a time for discovering our abilities to express ideas, thoughts, and opinions, and to engage in individual, family, community, and global projects. Students return to the classroom to enrich their education. Autumn, like all the other seasons, is also a time for growing. As we realize the fruits of our labor, we are now ready to hunt, research, and pursue new goals and dreams. The third chapter, subtitled "Harvest," is a gathering of ideas that challenge the writer to develop logical/mathematical and verbal/linguistic expression.

Winter brings us to an awareness that I like to think of as "walking in balance." It is a time for inner exploration and healing. It is a time for becoming more grounded, for spreading one's roots, and for engaging in self-nurturing activities. The fourth chapter offers tools for enhancing all forms of expression.

Each chapter of *Writing with Multiple Intelligences* begins with educational, psychological, and spiritual insights I have gleaned from various sources. It is my hope that these insights will inspire you to tap into your own creativity and to explore your own and your students' multiple intelligences. In the following three sections, I provide some background on the major sources of these insights.

The Creative Connection Process: Natalie Rogers

I like to think of the creative process as a dynamic spiral, which is beautifully illustrated in Natalie Rogers' model of the "creative connection process." (See Figures 1 and 2 from Rogers's *The Creative Connection Process.*)

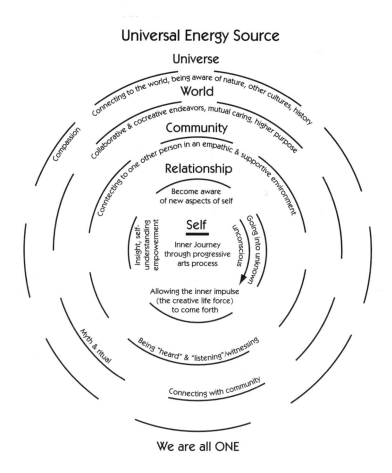

Universal Energy Source

Universe

World

Community

Relationship

Self

We are all ONE

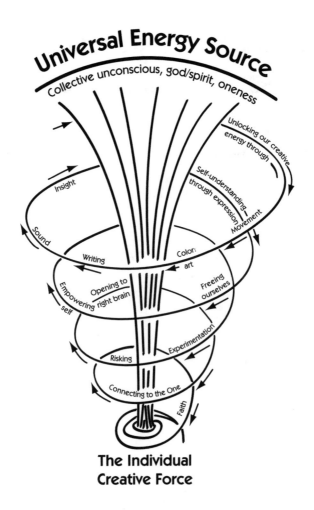

**The Individual
Creative Force**

According to Natalie Rogers, as we first journey inward through the expressive arts, we tap into the unconscious and become aware of new aspects of the self, thus gaining personal insight and empowerment. Then, by connecting to at least one person in an empathic and supportive environment, we develop ways to relate to the community. As we learn how to be authentic and empowered in a small community, we are inspired to move to the larger circle. We become co-creative and collaborative, and are able to access our highest purpose and powers. This process allows us to connect to the world—and to other cultures and nature—with compassion.

Rogers further suggests that by moving from art form to art form, we release layers of inhibitions, bringing us to our center—our individual creative force. This center opens us to the universal energy source, which awakens vitality and a sense of oneness.

Whether working with gifted and talented or at-risk populations, I find that the creative and expressive arts possess healing powers. In order for healing and change to occur, we have to be willing to take risks—to shape our dreams and visions as we explore our own potential for creative expression through writing. Hardships can become precious lessons. As long as we keep going, we open ourselves up to more and more of life (and ultimately to ourselves). At the same time, studying the self ultimately frees the self. For example, once I have given birth to a poem, it takes on a life of its own. Jung wrote that achieving a state of self-realization depends largely upon the ego making conscious that which is unconscious. The practices of writing poetry, painting a picture, playing a musical instrument, and dancing are all forms of creative expression that lead to self-awareness.

There is an ancient haiku, written by Izumu Shikibu (974?–1034?), which illustrates the sense of oneness that is attained when tapping into the universal energy source:

I cannot say
which is which
the glowing
plum blossom *is*
the spring night's moon.

Flow: Csikszentmihalyi

According to Csikszentmihalyi, "The metaphor of *flow* is one that many people have used to describe the sense of effortless action they feel in moments that stand out as the best in their lives. Athletes refer to it as 'being in the zone,' religious mystics as being in 'ecstasy,' artists and musicians as aesthetic rapture. Athletes, mystics, and artists do very different things when they reach flow, yet their descriptions are remarkably similar." For me, flow is at its best when I am challenged to make leaps into new realms of thinking. Flow does not come to me when I am bored or when I am distracted by inner or outer noise. Deadlines often enhance my productivity, and thus facilitate optimum performance. I experience flow when I have a clear goal, such as baking bread or planting bulbs.

Flow moves through the chapters of my book as I describe the process of entering into a state of stillness and concentration—freeing the mind of all distractions and worries—in order to write. While many creative thinkers and artists rely upon their environment as a source of inspiration, I find that I can write anywhere, as long as I am able to devote full attention to my mind and body. The laundromat, airplanes, waiting rooms in doctors' offices, the car as it's getting filled up with gas. These are not places noted for their glamor, but they do provide time and the opportunity to put my thoughts into words if I am in flow.

I become one with the creative act when I am most grounded and present in the moment. I had such an experience at the closing ceremony of a doctoral seminar on "Professional and Personal Stress Transformation" that I attended in November 1996 at the Kripalu Yoga Center in

Lenox, Massachusetts. There I was asked to read my poetry, accompanied by the bamboo flute improvisations of one of our instructors, Jonathan Foust. The simplicity and stillness of the landscape invited me to enter into a state of flow, which I then put into words:

AUTUMN IN THE ENDLESS MOUNTAINS

> What is this pure music?
> Wings of leaves
> floating down.
> Horses graze in crystal hues
> of frost-lit fields.
> I stare into their eyes
> and feel my fears disappear.
> Gulls soar in the cliffs.
> I don't know where I'm going.
> I've never been here before.
> I'll keep walking.
> Something inside of me knows
> that beyond the rough and rocky terrain
> there will be still waters.
> On the hillside,
> the woman picking apples
> is a prayer.
> Filled with odors of wood smoke,
> day breaks across an open canvas
> my own heart climbs through.

I am learning to take the concept of flow with me wherever I go. I invite you to join me on this journey by engaging in the writing exercises provided herein.

Edna Kovacs
May 6, 2000

CHAPTER ONE

Spring: Beginner's Mind—A Time for Budding

APRIL IN HOOD RIVER, OREGON

When I think of how to begin again
already the dark buds are forming.

I compare myself to these lilacs—
heavy with blossoms on every bough.

Stalwart limbs
remember.

My winter is over.
I will continue to grow.

Body/Kinesthetic Intelligence

Movement wakens the senses. Making the mind-body connection offers profound ways to engage in psycho-physical work while exploring creative expression. This section offers ways to bring body/kinesthetic intelligence to life.

1. The Dance

Of all the uses of the body, none has reached greater heights than the dance.

　　　　　—Howard Gardner

How does it feel to be a circle? A square? A triangle? A tree? The ocean? The wind or the rain? Learn or make up dance steps and create words for them, suggests David Lazear in his *Eight Ways of Knowing*. Create human sculpture tableaux. Act out a story. Role-play. Videotape performances. These are all ways of activating creative expression through movement.

An example of Hawaiian hula dance, "Sweet Leilani," illustrates the potential for creative expression through non-verbal communication. I invite my students to learn the movements and then write about how the dance makes them feel in what-

Sweet Leilani
Ka'o right, left. Hands at head then gracefully move to hips.

heavenly flower
Kaholo right. Hands pick flower and shape bud.

I dreamed of paradise
Kaholo left. Hands in dream position.

for two
Ka'o right, left. Two fingers, right hand, left hand on hip.

You are my paradise
Kaholo right. Hands pointing to right.

completed
Kaholo left. Hands open and cross over chest in embrace.

you are my dreams
Kaholo right. Hands in dream position.

come true
Step back on left foot, point right foot... Hands come from self forward and open palms up, palms down...

ever genre is theirs.

Danskinetics and yoga are also wonderful ways to use kinesthetic expression as a form of haptic[1] communication. Movement, stretching, and breathing help unlock blocked emotions, while silent meditation followed by journal writ-

...and bow.

[1] *Haptic* comes from the Greek *haptikos,* which means "the ability to grasp, sense, or perceive." (From *The Random House Dictionary of the English Language,* Second Edition).

ing can fill you with a sense of strength and inner peace.

At home, I listen to different kinds of music—popular, classical, folk, jazz, and new age—and let the music move me from the inside–out. Dance is a wonderful release for all my feelings, as well as a catalyst for self-expression. Tensions are released. My body feels rejuvenated. Afterwards, I find myself re-energized to write. When I teach writing with music workshops for young children, I ask the children to move like different animals, seasons, feelings, shapes, and colors. Afterwards, we write poems, draw pictures, and create songs and skits. Movement has enabled my students and me to discover the healing powers of the expressive arts.

2. Changing Awareness through Breathing and Walking

I have had great success doing this writing exercise with high school and college students. As a field trip or homework assignment, this activity gives students the opportunity to discover that writing is as natural as breathing.

The following transfer strategy from David Lazear is one in which you and your students can experiment with shifting your awareness to deal with situations you encounter in daily life. It involves the conscious use of breathing and walking. The imagery in this exercise is taken from various Medicine Wheel traditions. It uses the four cardinal directions and the four basic elements. Students should walk in the direction indicated in parenthesis as they meditate. Work with each of the following four sections until you sense the change it can bring about in your awareness. Conclude each section by writing.

[NOTE: You may find that if you close your eyes during the "Breathe" parts of the exercise it is easier to imagine what is suggested and that the results/effects are more noticeable.]

THE EARTH (West)
RESTORES A SENSE OF STABILITY AND GROUNDEDNESS

Breathe: Breathe in and out through your nose. Think of the earth below you. As you breathe in, imagine you can draw the earth's life-giving energy up your spine. As you breathe out, feel yourself attracted to the earth beneath, like you are being drawn by a magnet. Continue breathing in this way as you start to walk.

Walk: As you walk, be very aware of where your feet are going. Place them exactly where you want them. Walk with purpose and intention. Walk as if there was a strong hand behind you, supporting you. This is the walk of an irresistible force. Nothing can stop you!

Pause for a moment and think of a situation in your life that needs this kind of walk—purposeful, grounded, clear in direction. Now begin walking again, imagining or visualizing yourself walking into that situation with the walk of the Earth.

> Walking in copper rain
> I feel myself becoming
> a woman again

THE WATER (South)
RESTORES A SENSE OF OPENNESS, FLEXIBILITY, AND LOVE

Breathe: Breathe in through your nose and out through your mouth, your lips just slightly parted. Imagine that the breath is a fine stream of cleansing water flowing through you. Feel the clean, fresh flow as you become the water of life. Continue breathing in this way as you start the walk.

Walk: Walk with great sensitivity and great gentleness. Walk as though you are walking on soft grass in your bare feet. Walk "in tune" with everything around you, like a deer in the forest—totally aware, harmless, and at one with the environment. There is no self: you are in harmony with everything.

Pause for a moment and think of a situation in your life that needs this kind of walk—flexible, open, compassionate. Now begin walking again, imagining or visualizing yourself walking into that situation with the walk of water.

SPRING NIGHT

> Chambray dusk
> harbinger of darkness
> apogee moon rises
> filling the silence.
> Mellifluent stars illuminate
> jade cliffs
> hanging nests.
> The shore is empty now—
> but for a few enduring
> paw tracks, quells of kelp
> supine driftwood.
> Omen of yare winds
> luff against limbs of
> wind-twisted cypresses.

Rising from sleeping reeds
in the scented breeze
tantaras of smoky gray sea gulls.

THE FIRE (EAST)

RESTORES ENERGY, WILL, CONFIDENCE, AND MOTIVATION FOR ACTION

Breathe: Breathe deeply, in through your mouth and out through your nose. Imagine that each inhalation blows on hot coals in your solar plexus. On the exhalation, feel the energy from this fire radiating throughout your body. Sense this energy pouring out from you in all directions. Continue breathing in this way as you start the walk.

Walk: As you walk, imagine the sun in your heart. Let this energy drive your walk. Become a torch so bright and full of light that all darkness disappears. Walk with clear vision, like a sunbeam or a ray of bright light. Set your sights on where you want to go and walk straight for that point with confidence, courage, and no sense of limitation.

Pause for a moment and think of a situation in your life that needs this kind of walk—confident, clearly directed, passionate. Now begin walking again, imagining or visualizing yourself walking into that situation with the walk of fire.

ARROYO

Leaving the world behind
aspens glow
in this deepening cosmos.

Here, nothing seems to matter
but for the light that dances
from rock to rock like a flame
throughout the canyon.

I just get the feeling
with each step and
every breath—
all is sacred.

The whole land
resonates with sage.
An autumn breeze reminds me
of the great ocean.

Of the people
whose faces remain
among the red clay and rimrock.
Their voices rise like jays

into the long dust that blows
in all directions:
a patina of juniper
purple aster
Indian paintbrush.

Clouds feather.
In the red of chinle,
a spider weaves
her ancient melody.
Chamisa bow their heads
as waves rise up
to meet me
in dusk's translucent
dreamlight.

THE AIR (NORTH)
RESTORES INNER VISION, INTUITION, AND CONNECTION WITH ALL ABOVE
THE EARTH

Breathe: Breathe in and out through your mouth, your lips barely parted, and your breath very refined. Use the exhalation to blow your mind, thoughts, and emotions way out into the universe. Use the inhalation to bring your mind, thoughts, and emotions back together again. Then blow them out again. Continue breathing in this way as you start the walk.

Walk: Focus your full attention on a point 8–10 inches above your head and begin to walk. This is like floating or flying. You're not sure how you get from one place to another. It's like being transported. Walk without any intention—just follow your intuition. Feel yourself expanding in all directions. Let yourself become vast and all-encompassing.

Pause for a moment and think of a situation in your life that needs this kind of walk—vast, panoramic, full of insight. Now begin walking again, imagining or visualizing yourself walking into that situation with the walk of air.

FOR GRASS VALLEY, OREGON

Today I dream myself awake
walking through sage-scented hills.
I will get lost
where the hawk glides
where the moon's silver legato
slips between the pines.

In this universe
talk is made up of cricket syllables
hoof beats of wild horses
tumbleweed tales and barn owl parables
April wheat waving in the wind.

3. Similes

Regardless of what time of the school year it is, young children enjoy being engaged in kinesthetic learning activities. I like to lead students in kindergarten through fifth grade in the following simile-writing and movement exercise which explores writing from the body in a dynamic way. Teachers will want to give students plenty of space for this exercise. I suggest using a stage, playground, or gym.

Give students a list of the beginnings of similes (e.g. "Trees move like...") and ask them to come up with the second parts. Once the students have created their lists, have them decide which of their similes they would like to act out. They can work individually or in small groups. This is kinesthetic and collaborative learning at its best! I have been amazed at how the shy new students can lose their inhibitions and join in the fun. The following similes were written and performed by a second grade student during an after-school workshop I led at Sweetbriar Elementary School in Troutdale, Oregon, in the winter of 2000 (through the Regional Arts & Culture Council's Neighborhood Arts Program and the Eastwind Center):

Trees move like a whimpering willow.
Sun looks like a big orange bouncing ball.
Moon seems like the sun's husband.

River is shaped like a loooooooooonnnnnnggg
  sucker.
Stars feel like a razor sharp sword.
Oceans are like milkshakes.
Rainbows bend like rubber bands.
Earth is like a face. The continents are its eyes
  and the water flowing through is its mouth.
Wind whispers like a wombat.
Rain falls like tears falling from the sky.
Gold shines like the rays of the sun.
Glaciers glide like snowboards and birds.
Day begins like a bird's sweet sound of
  tweeting.
Night ends like an owl's hoot and a bat's
  screech.

§

Happy as an alien
Mad as a lion
Ferocious as a rhinoceros
Scared as a frog
Wild as a monkey
Kind as a kitten
Surprised as a gorilla
Sad as a pug dog
Fast as a cheetah
Strong as an elephant
Nice as a cat
Tall as a giraffe
Round as a fat guy
Sharp as a nail
Silent as a mouse
Old as a toad
  —Tim Chase

4. Writing from the Body

Writing from the body is a dance of trust and timing. As John Lee puts it in *Writing from the Body*, "For many of us, stilling the mind is like trying to seize lightning. Sitting still can be more difficult. If you find physical stillness challenging, seek out a form of movement that quiets your mental lawnmower. Take long walks. Work in the garden. Practice yoga. When you return from your mind-cleansing activity, your body will glide into each sentence, and your breath will inspire each word."

John Lee suggests the following exercise for waking the Muse:

> *Try any kind of movement you enjoy—walk with a brisk step, run somewhere, dance to some favorite music, swim a few laps, whatever your body likes. While you're moving, let songs and scenes, memories, emotions, sentences and paragraphs, poems, even unintelligible sounds, arise inside you as you move. Listen attentively, and with love. Trust that when you return to your desk, you'll remember the essentials. When you arrive home, whatever remains in your memory is a gift of the Muse. Accept it and enjoy it. Swim in it as you would an early morning dream. When you awaken, the details you remember are yours.*

If I feel blocked or full, rather than sit and stare at a blank computer screen, I engage in kinesthetic movement such as stretching, yoga, danskinetics, deep breathing, or taking a long walk. I find that these are profoundly effective ways to make a mental clearing and deepen my vision.

The following poem, written in Lincoln City (at the Oregon coast), illustrates how I can experience the creative process through movement:

TABLE BY THE SEA

I stayed awake half the night
dreaming of a table by the sea.
Yesterday, I sat for hours
making studies of figures, faces—
A window was the most
intimate object within that picture.
I went home restless
in despair of that canvas.
Nearly noon, the shutters
burst open, bringing in
the smell of fish. Salt-mist
shaded sea-cliffs
cries of gulls intersected
penciled rhythms
against a gray horizon.
I considered the objects on
the table: a bowl of apples
and empty vase, sheets of music—
When I touched the strings
of my guitar, notes rose
clear, connected.
The dim candle rushed from wall
to wall, breathing on to a page
of half-awake sketches.
In my curiosity, I ran outside. I
began to remember my legs and
body. I ran until I lost
my breath—until I became
a part of that landscape of
waves racing one against another
becoming one triumphant form.
They were not statues,

not vacuous, not skeletons.
Their living peaks rose up
again and again.
Light threw itself upon them—
changing ideas about transparency.
When green clouds of foam
touched heels of waves, they resonated
in tones of turquoise-silver:
a scherzo in blue and gray.
Hours later, when I returned
to my room, I saw the objects
on the table as companions.
Now I could paint them.

Interpersonal Intelligence

Collaborative writing is a resourceful way to engage students with each other and promote creative communication. Interpersonal learning activities have the potential to entrust individuals within a group, and the group as a whole, with a shared vision of the creative process. Shared projects like the ones represented in this section demonstrate how writing together can strengthen a group's sense of community.

The ideas put forth in this chapter are group-oriented. Examples of student work are included from residencies and workshops I have led through the Regional Arts & Culture Council's Neighborhood Arts Program, the Oregon Council for the Humanities' Chautauqua-in-the-Schools, the Oregon State Poetry Association in association with the Oregon State Library and Oregon Community Foundation, and

Young Audiences of Oregon. Participants in these workshops were of all ages and walks of life.

1. Linked Verse Writing from Korea

From ancient to modern times, linked verse writing has engaged people to explore a collective point of view on varied topics. Linked verse writing may extend across the curriculum. Anything, from a piece of music to a scientific topic to a current event, may be used as the catalyst for the exercise.

In May of 2000, I taught linked verse writing to seventh-grade students at Fernwood Middle School in Portland, Oregon. It is helpful with elementary and middle school students to create lead phrases and prompts for each topic. For example, at Fernwood we created linked verse around the theme of unity. We brainstormed to come up with topics that students could choose from, such as compassion, family, friendship, loyalty, peace, trust, and a question about unity. Based on these topics, we created the following prompts:

Compassion: I feel compassion towards…
Family: I wish my family would…
Friendship: Things that I look for in a friend are…;
    and things that make me a good friend are…
Loyalty: I am loyal to…
Peace: Peace is nurtured when…
Trust: Things that build trust are…
Question and Answer: What is unity?

Working in groups of four, each student then selected a topic from the list, wrote it at the top of his or her piece of paper, and wrote several lines of poetry or prose about the topic. When they were finished writing, each student passed his or her piece of paper to the left. Students then wrote several lines about the topics that had been passed to them. Topics made two full circulations through the group. Often, circulating the resulting compositions among the group more than once deepens the written output considerably. We then created *acrostic* poems about unity, and shared our poems aloud. (See the "Writing about Nature" section of this chapter for an example of an acrostic poem.)

The following example of linked verse writing was written by five young fifteenth-century scholars from the Hall of Worthies. They were granted a leave of absence to study at the Chin'gwan Monastery on Mount Samgak.

UPON LISTENING TO THE FLUTE (1442)

Where does it come from, the sound of a flute,
At midnight on a blue-green peak?
Song Sam-mun

Shaking the moonlight, it rings high,
Borne by the wind, it carries far.   *Yi Kae*

Clear and smooth like a warbler's song,
The floating melody rolls downhill.
Pak P'aeng-nyon

Always, ever, a lover looks in the mirror,
And amid vibrant silence, night deepens in the
hills.
Yi Sok-hyung

Splitting a stone, limpid notes are stout,
"Plucking a Willow Branch" breaks a lover's
heart.[1]   *Song Sam-mun*

---

1. This is accompanied by a horizontal flute; so is "Plum Blossoms Fall" nine lines later.

Clear and muddy notes come in order,
the kung and shang modes unmixed.² *Yi Kae*

How wonderful, notes drawn out and released,
How pleasant, reaping waves of sound.

Long since I played it seated on my bed.
Where is the zestful player leaning against the
tower?

Pak P'aeng-nyon

Marvelous melodies recall Ts'ai Yen,
Who remembers Juan Chi's clear whistle?

Yi Sok-hyong

"Plum Blossoms Fall" in the garden,
Fishes and dragons fight in the deep sea.

Song Sam-mun

First, the drawn out melody startled me,
Now I rejoice in the clear, sweet rhythm. *Yi Kae*

How can only a reed whistle in Lung
Make the Tartar traders flee, homesick?

Shin Suk-Chu

On Mount Kou-shih a phoenix calls limpidly,
In the deep pool a dragon hums and dances.

Pak P'aeng-nyon

A wanderer is struck homesick over the pass,
A widow pines in her room.   *Yi Sok-hyong*

Floating, floating, the music turns sad,
Long, long, my thought is disquieted.

Song Sam-mun

2. *Kung* and *shang* are the first two notes of a pentatonic scale.

We were all ears at the first notes,
But can't grasp the dying sounds.   *Yi Kae*

A startled wind rolls away the border sands,
Cold snow drives though Ch'in park.
                                        Shin Suk-chu

I don't tire of your music,
Should I rise and dance to your tune?
                                        Pak P'aeng-nyon

Who is that master flautist,
His creative talent all his own.   *Yi Sok-hyung*

Prince Chi'ao is really not dead,
Has Huan I returned from the underworld?
                                        Song Sam-mun

His solo—a whoop of a single crane,
In unison—a thousand ox-drawn carriages.
                                        Yi Kae

Choking, choking, now a tearful complaint,
Murmuring, murmuring, now a tender whisper.
                                        Shin Suk-chu

I beg you, flute master,
Hide your art, don't spoil it.   *Yi Sok-hyung*

Confucius heard Shao and lost his taste for
    meat;
I too forget to take my meal.   *Pak P'eng-nyon*

I cannot help cherishing your art,
I set forth my deep love for you! *Song Sam-mun*

The next example was written by my adult creative class at Metropolitan Learning Center's Community Schools during the fall of 1988.

OBLATION

The sharp edge of suffering has not entered my
    family through
the door of AIDS. I slam the door and hold it
    tight but moans and
sighs penetrate.   *Shirley Gifford*

Am I afraid of getting what you got
or am I afraid you'll see me needing
something you have to give?
                          Kathleen B. Goldberg

Why the fear? But
who is free of it?
It lurks like a shadow behind
everything, corrupts all
possible intimacy.   *Emery Hermans*
Plans, dreams never fulfilled. A life not lived;
Death is never just; it comes leaving sadness
in its wake.   *Monica Schelb*

You lay dormant so long.
If only we had realized your slumber was
death in waiting.
Now you lie among us, your trademarks
emaciation, weakness, pain.
                          Clarissa M. Dearmon

Night flowers fade
I feel the wind mourn for you—
don't blame yourself for being human.

Edna Kovacs

My wish to soothe and help
Is in conflict with my urge to ignore the cries
and remain safely apart.   *Michael O'Hara*

I keep hoping it will just go away
and it doesn't
and it won't until
the hatred that feeds it
dies.   *Douglas Dunlap*

Can we work together to end this dark chaos,
Interconnect medical science with man's hope
    and unite
so that one day we may all bathe in Eternal
    light?

Maurice LaFollette

If students are still having difficulty getting started after I share these examples, I ask them to mind-map or list their current events. That is, I ask them to answer the question: "What's going on for you right now?" Nouns. Verbs. Adjectives. People. Feelings. Colors. The ball gets rolling. And once it does…!

This engaging mode of writing is a wonderful tool for enhancing self-expression through a shared-responsibility approach. You may wish to try writing linked verses on topics across the curriculum. Teens will love to write about personal interests such as cars, fashion, music, and sports.

2. The Story Circle

You don't have anything if you don't have the stories.
—Leslie Silko

Native American tradition offers a delightful way to share experiences aloud. Using a special talisman, a stone, or a feather, you can germinate ideas for writing by sharing stories aloud. The talisman is passed to each person in a circle; whoever holds the talisman at a given time is the storyteller.

Barry Lane, who has taught writing in prisons, public schools, colleges, and literary programs, suggests the following activity in his *Writing as a Road to Self-Discovery*:

> *Finding themes is a natural process that comes after we have told many stories. So let's tell a few stories. Invite family or good friends for a story night. You are going to teach them a Native American ritual called the* story circle. *Western European society's ritual is called* conversation. *That's where you tell me about the time you totaled your first Chevy, and I butt in and say, "That reminds me of the time I wrecked my VW...." With a story circle only one person talks—the person with the* talking stick. *A talking stick can be anything from a pen to an elaborately carved cane. I suggest finding something that has some meaning to you. Once everyone is sitting in a circle, pass the stick around and have people start telling stories.*

Here are a few prompts that I've found to be wonderful for dredging up core stories and jump-starting story circles with students of all ages. Some of these contain themes that could be considered core stories in and of themselves. When issuing a prompt, always leave the storyteller the option of just telling any old story. The goal is to tell stories, not fulfill assignments.

A time you ran away (doesn't have to be just physically)
A time you escaped
A first time doing something
A time that was horrible then, but you laugh about now
The day you were no longer a child
An encounter with death
A time you did something that you shouldn't have
A time you did something that you were proud of
A time you were mystified
A time you were confused
A time you lost something (anything) forever
A time you discovered something
A time you were terrified
A time something happened that confirmed something
    for you
A time you were in awe
A time you came home

Each person tells a story and the others listen and write questions about the story on scraps of paper. When the storyteller is through with his or her story, the questions are passed to the teller and are put into an envelope for later.

Let the talisman or stick go around and around until everyone has told several stories. Explain to people that they don't *have* to tell a story when they receive the stick, but ask them to hold the stick for a few seconds to see if a story will come to them. Because this is a circle, the stick will eventually come back to them if they pass.

1. When all the stories are told, everyone looks at the questions that the others passed to them. Each person should pick the question that pulls at him or her most. Then, they turn it into a lead by simply answering it. For example:

"What were you doing there?" could be answered with the lead, "I didn't know what I was doing there."

2. Have the students freewrite for twenty minutes following the lead and then stop to reread what they have written.

3. Have them put the writing aside. Prompt students to close their eyes and imagine the stories they wrote about. Tell them to think of the place and to put themselves back there.

4. Now ask them to open their eyes and list twenty details that they remember. A detail is simply a piece of information. It can be one word, like "big," or a sentence or two, like, "My father sits in the corner eating pistachio nuts and watching a heavyweight prizefight."

5. Then have the students make their details more specific by asking questions about each one. Tell them to think of themselves as turning the knob on their binoculars to create a clearer picture. They should write the revised details next to the original details.

6. Ask them to pick one detail from their list and start on a new page. Have them freewrite about the event starting with the chosen detail. Tell them to feel free to stray away from the subject if they want to.

7. Have them reread what they've written and write one sentence that sums up a common theme between the two freewrites.

8. Have them write one question they would still like to answer about their subject.

Digging Deeper

Ask the following questions to go deeper: Were there any similarities between the questions others passed to you? Did you discover any surprising details when you answered the questions? Did you uncover any common themes in your story that relate to other stories that you have told or other events in your life?

Links to Curriculum

In Oregon, I use the story circle to structure my presentation on storytelling about place. I work with students to find themes relating to Northwest regionalism, such as people, places, or natural phenomena. The use of a story circle also serves as a catalyst for writing and research projects or other creative endeavors in which the class may engage. The potential links to curriculum are numerous. The learning that takes place is experiential and taps into writing with multiple intelligences on a number of different levels. You may also choose to polish and videotape your story circles so that they become performances.

3. Calendar Poetry

"Through Our Own Eyes"

The following are selections from an art and poetry calendar that was created by students at Roosevelt High School in Portland, Oregon. This ARTSPLAN 2000 + project was funded by the Regional Arts & Culture Council and Young Audiences of Oregon, Inc. in 1996.

For ten weeks, twice a week, I worked with sophomore students in Arts and Communication and ESL programs. Together we explored forms of multicultural poetry such as the ghazal, haiku, calligramme, and waka from my book *Writing Across Cultures: A Handbook for Writing Poetry & Lyrical Prose* (Blue Heron Publishing, Inc., Hillsboro, OR: 1994), Shelley Tucker's *Painting the Sky* (GoodYear Books, Glenview, IL: 1995), and Jack Canfield and Harold Wells's *100 Ways to Enhance Self-Concept in the Classroom* (Prentice-Hall, Inc., Englewood Cliffs, NJ: 1976).

Not only did the students enjoy immersing themselves in learning how to write the blues, ghazal, and haiku, but they also appreciated listening to the musical examples I brought in from the many cultures we explored. Over the course of the semester their portfolios burgeoned with their own creativity. Their ability to express themselves improved dramatically, as did their self-concepts and their capacities to work collaboratively on writing projects.

At the end of the semester, students produced polished portfolios for credit, and, under the artistic direction of publisher Dennis Stovall, formed an editorial committee to publish a school calendar that was funded by the district. Local businesses supported the project with ads, and the students were able to sell the calendar for four dollars each. Funds were used to buy the first computers and software for student use in Roosevelt's history. As the poetry instructor, I was uplifted to see such initiative, pride, and growth among under-served youth.

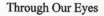

Through Our Eyes

1997

Arts and Communications Class
Roosevelt High School

Fugue

Pity **is the color of dying orange**
Pity **wishes for closure**
Pity **moves cautiously**
Pity **wears a boy's haircut**
Pity **shows us how not to be**
Pity **has a pocket full of scorn**

> –Lorraine-Michelle Lanausse-Faust
> and Jennifer Keeland

Chaos is the color of politics.
Chaos wishes for expansion.
Chaos moves like nature.
Chaos wears invisible clothes.
Chaos shows us beauty.
Chaos has a pocket of humanity.

-Matt Grant

Linked Verse

HATE

Hate is something I often feel.
It hits me like a disease.
Hate makes me lonely.
Wishing for love.
Hate makes me sick.
The dislike of something or someone. .
Hate is very strong.
It hits and rips the heart.
Hate can be good, but mostly bad.
In the end, it always makes me sad.

GeorgAnnette Chatterley,
JaVonda Dillon,
Sharlene Morgan
and
Angela Toedtemeier,

Blues

Livin' in the 'hood'
Livin' in the 'hood
Sometimes it ain't all good

I always carry a knife
I always carry a knife
for all these baseheads tryin' to take my life.

Seein' all these bums
Seein' all these bums
with a bottle gripped tight with their thumbs

Peepin' around the corner wherever I go
Peepin' around the corner wherever I go
Y'all who don't live in the hood just don't know

-Jeremy Bufton

Shrinking

"Dreams Were Made To Be Caught"

A fantasy I enjoy is I wish I could sing a beckoning
song in a form fitting dress on top of a grand piano.
-Jennifer Keeland

The web that I now weave
should catch my dreams.
What a way I would
have with me.

But what dream
would I catch?
A great romance, that's it
Maybe it would be tragic
Or maybe an uncommon circumstance
where we were meant to be.
With all things that a
romance should have.
Tragedy, lust, determined to be
With your one true love.

I have another dream that
Would be worth catching.
To travel, what an adventure.
I'd go to a forbidden place
One where deadly choices
Await.

But there needs to be
Something worth the while.
Maybe a beautiful valley
With harmony.

I shall keep these dreams in
my feathers so that I may dream them once again.

-Inga Cusic

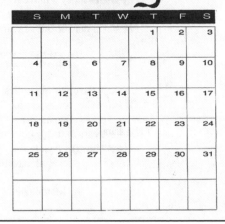

Identity

S	M	T	W	T	F	S
				1	2	3
4	5	6	7	8	9	10
11	12	13	14	15	16	17
18	19	20	21	22	23	24
25	26	27	28	29	30	31

Earth Poem

WATER

I cover most of the planet
I'm a necessity of life for all
Without me, all would die
I can fit through the tiniest hole
yet fill an entire ocean
I'm worshipped for my effect on everything
I can give life but I can also take it away
just as fast
The sun steals me
yet
worst of all
I'm polluted by man
Love me
Clean me
Don't destroy me

-Scott Winklebleck

JULY

S	M	T	W	T	F	S
		1	2	3	4	5
6	7	8	9	10	11	12
13	14	15	16	17	18	19
20	21	22	23	24	25	26
27	28	29	30	31		

People Like Me Because...

I don't care.

I am funny.

I listen.

I make people smile.

I am fun to hang out with.

I give someone one of my smiles if they don't
have one of their own.

I make them laugh

group poem

Haiku

in the summer time
the weather is really hot
daylight last longer

-Angela Knight

blue periwinkles
brightly colored other life
floating through the creek

-Laura Sharp

The watermelons
are very sweet and juicy.
Juice drips down my face.

-Angela Knight

AUGUST

S	M	T	W	T	F	S
					1	2
3	4	5	6	7	8	9
10	11	12	13	14	15	16
17	18	19	20	21	22	23
24	25	26	27	28	29	30
31						

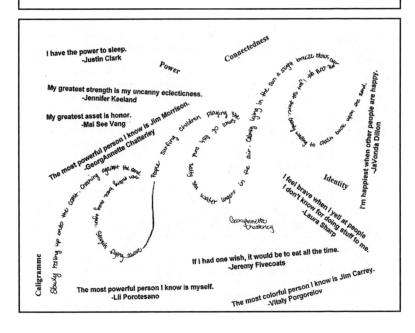

I have the power to sleep.
-Justin Clark

Power

Connectedness

My greatest strength is my uncanny eclecticness.
-Jennifer Keeland

My greatest asset is honor.
-Mai See Vang

The most powerful person I know is Jim Morrison.
-GeorgAnnette Chatterley

Identity

I feel brave when I yell at people I don't know for doing stuff to me.
-Laura Sharp

I'm happiest when other people are happy.
-JaVonda Dillon

If I had one wish, it would be to eat all the time.
-Jeremy Fivecoats

The most powerful person I know is myself.
-Lil Porotesano

The most colorful person I know is Jim Carrey.
-Vitaly Porgorelov

Caligramme

50

4. Poetry and Art as Therapy

Healing through the Creative Process
"Something from All of Us"

You can also have groups of students create poetry and art books. The following excerpts are from such a project, created by at-risk women and runaway teenagers at the Eastwind Center in Gresham, Oregon. The workshops I conducted there were made possible by funds from the Regional Arts & Culture Council's Neighborhood Arts Program and from Multnomah County's Department of Community and Family Services. During the production of this collection, the participants came to realize that self-expression through art and poetry can be both healing and empowering. As Gabriel Rico puts it, "Healing and creativity are two sides of the same coin."

Something from All of Us

Blue

Blue is the color of the sky
when it shines above me.
Blue is the feeling that I feel
when I am down.
Blue is a beautiful color
which always seems to attract
my attention.
Blue is the ocean
when it moves slowly towards
land.
Blue is the chilly feeling
in the cold.
Blue is the gum that I like
to chew.
Blue are the
confusing moments I am
feeling right now.

Xiomara

I Have the Power to...

Make people feel

Make people feel better about themselves

Change

Care

Think

Give

To enjoy life or be miserable

Give company to people

Make people laugh

group poem

If I Had One Wish It Would Be...

TO LIVE IN DISNEYLAND

To become Goofy

To live the life I choose

TO HAVE MORE TIME FOR FUN

**To see Jeremy so I
   can say "I love you" and "Good-bye."**

To find the Genie's magic lamp.

To have my best friend alive again.

group poem

5. Imagination Hat

The following community writing project, created on November 8, 1997, in Cascade Locks, Oregon, was made possible by a grant from the Oregon State Poetry Association, the Oregon Community Foundation, the Oregon State Library, and the Edna Holmes Foundation. Everyone in the daylong gathering, people ranging in ages from six to eighty, welcomed the following warm-up suggestion for introducing metaphor and imagery. I call it "Imagination Hat."

Have you ever noticed how clouds sometimes take on the shapes of rabbits, mushrooms, or flying fish? Take a look at the world around you. If you're wearing your imagination cap, you'll be able to suspend your belief in reality and re-visualize windows, doors, pencils, numbers, and clocks as other objects.

Several years ago, I had the opportunity to work with writer Jim Heynen at the Northwest Writing Institute through Lewis and Clark College's Writers at Home in Oregon Libraries program. To begin a prewriting activity with third- and fourth-grade students, Jim tossed his cap into the air and began by asking, "A hat is not a hat—what else does it look like?" He instructed the students to put on their imagination caps.

"A hat is not a hat. It's a flying saucer!" one child said.

"And if I open it up and start picking strawberries, what is it then?" Jim asked.

"It's a basket for picking strawberries."

What else does a triangle look like? The number *8*? The letter *V*? A triangle isn't a triangle; it's a slice of pizza with olives, mushrooms, and green peppers on it. The number *8* isn't the number *8*; it's a snowman. Turn it around sideways, and it's a pair of eyeglasses. The letter *V* isn't the letter *V*; it's the wings of a bird. An arabesque isn't an arabesque; it's a butterfly.

A good writer is attuned to his or her senses. Open your eyes. Tell us what you see. Discover the world of images. Students may wish to create shape poems or mobiles and share these poems aloud.

A cloud
is not a cloud
it's a bowl of ice cream.   *Ann Holmstrom*

A planet
is not a planet
it is a basketball.   *Peter Holmstrom*

A mushroom
isn't a mushroom
it's a person standing
with an umbrella.   *Sara Curl*

The moon
isn't the moon
it's a cookie in the sky.   *Joseph Nolin*

A book
is not a book
it is a passport.   *June Knudsen*

A plant
is not a plant
it's a drinking straw.   *Laura Rush*

A car
is not a car
it's my dad.   *Jenna Rush*

A pine tree
is not a pine tree.
It's a paintbrush with its
bristles all spread out.   *Ashley Mount*

You can also have students do this activity with partners. One partner begins the poem, and the other creates the refrain. I like to engage the group by using an image with a number of possibilities. A triangle can be a piece of pizza, a pyramid, and a tent. A cloud can be almost anything!

Now your students are ready to *become* something else. Have them write from the point of view of an object, an animal, or something in nature. They can write in poetry or prose form. The exercise on personification in chapter 4 is an excellent follow-up activity for this exercise. The following is a poem I wrote from the point of view of a flower:

PEONIES

It's as if my roots are telling me it's time.
This business of burying my head
in the ground is done.

Slowly, I rise.
My skirts grow wide
deepening into crimson.

First light
meets me
at the dancing grounds.

Naturalist Intelligence

By tapping into the naturalist intelligence, students are engaged to understand, appreciate, and enjoy the natural world. The creative writing suggestions included in this section are based upon the objectives described by David Lazear in *Seven Ways of Teaching*. In the introduction to a language arts lesson in his chapter on the naturalist intelligence, Lazear writes:

> *The natural world is full of innumerable things that can evoke the full range of our five senses as well as inner feelings, intuitions, memories, spiritual insight, and a profound sense of connectedness and unity. In lessons, students spend time in nature, allowing these things to be evoked within themselves. They then use this experience as a springboard to creative writing. They will focus on using their naturalist intelligence to help them deepen and enrich their writing. In addition to the naturalist intelligence, obviously verbal/linguistic intelligence also shares a secondary focus, for students will actually be writing about their experiences in nature. Intrapersonal intelligence "gets into the act," so to speak, as students are asked to become introspective and be aware of nature's impact on them via the traditional five senses, but also its effect on the "inner world" of the self.*

In several of the following exercises, students will be working with a partner, so interpersonal intelligence will also be involved. The language arts ideas include using nature-scene re-creations/simulations to stimulate the writing of prose and poetry, writing poetic/descriptive essays based on nature experiences, and creative story-writing using animal characters and their characteristics.

Teaching for and with the naturalist intelligence in the fine arts could include activities such as creative dancing that embodies patterns in nature or making collages and montages using leaves, pine cones, bark, moss, and other materials from nature.

1. Zen Poetry
Being in the Moment

These poems and meditations, often written in gusts of between five and fifteen per sitting, are meant to be handwritten on slips of paper and then hung willy-nilly on door jambs or window sills. They may be tied loosely to the limbs of a tree—wherever the wind can reach them. They should stay there until they are blown away or simply disappear.

The following two Zen poems are by Peter Levitt, a long-time teacher, poet, translator, and meditator in the Zen tradition.

within each petal
the sound of rain

* * *

In my garden
even the tallest sunflower
bows

The following is a Zen poem I wrote while exploring Stanley Park in Vancouver, British Columbia:

BLUE HERON

Leaving the path around
Burrard Bay, slick with
goose dung, I'm drawn
into a world of trees.
Leaves quake
with morning rain
black squirrels blink
between dark boughs.
The room widens into a ravine.
I follow the muddy footpath
to a serene autumn lake
where whirligigs flit
above beaver-eaten logs.
A fawn pauses in the reeds
sharing the secrecy
of water-lilies.
Suddenly, a whoosh of wings—
the lithe body and minaret neck
of a blue heron rising
her wings wide
across the water.

These clear reflections may be accompanied by brush-stroke paintings, watercolors, photographs, or music. I have listened to the music of the Japanese bamboo flute (shakuhachi) as a follow-up to writing in a garden or park, beside a waterfall or stream, or looking out a window.

2. Calligrammes
Shape Poems

Writing in nature may offer students the perfect opportunity to create poems in the shapes of what they see around them: trees, mountains, the sun, flowers, or birds. Students can make shape poems about what they see, smell, hear, taste, touch, and feel with partners or in small groups. Create calligrammes in all subject areas across the curriculum.

GUILLAUME APOLLINAIRE AND THE CALLIGRAMME

In *Sleeping on the Wing,* Kenneth Koch and Kate Farrell write:

> The French poet Guillaume Apollinaire lived and wrote at the end of the nineteenth and beginning of the twentieth century. He was killed in World War I. His lifetime corresponded with the beginning of the modern world, the world of automobiles, airplanes, electricity, and modern cities....And Apollinaire lived in Paris, the most beautiful city of the world, the city that was the center of art and science and thought, where it seemed that everything that mattered was going on. More than other poets, Apollinaire seemed to feel, and was able to express in his poems, the spirit and excitement of his time.
>
> New kinds of experience not only give the poets and other artists new subjects for their work, but also inspire them to find new forms for it, new ways of writing, and different ways of painting. The excitement about the modern did this in all the arts. The Cubist painters, for example, whom Apollinaire was friends with and whose

work he very much admired, painted pictures like none that he had ever seen before—showing things from different view-points at once, and full of angles and flatness, more like a modern street, than, say, a meadow. Like Cubist paintings, Apollinaire's work was new and unconventional. There's no punctuation; when there is rhyme, it is so light and flat it is hardly noticeable. Apollinaire's most obviously radical modern invention in poetry is the form he calls the calligramme *(the word seems related to Oriental picture-writing,* calligraphy, *and also to* telegram*). Instead of the usual shape of poetry, the poem has a shape determined by its subject. The letters of a love poem form the outline of a heart; the letters of a poem about rain fall like raindrops from the top to the bottom of the page. Such poems don't read like other poems, they don't even look like them.*

To write a calligramme, *begin with the shape of something and let that shape suggest to you what to write. For instance, if your poem is in the shape of clouds, let the clouds be the clouds of a certain day when you looked at them and thought and said and did certain things. A nice thing that happens in the writing of a* calligramme *is that the shape of the poem and the subject of the poem become mixed up and seem the same. You may want to write several.*

The following two examples of calligrammes, "Cat Moon" by Jannicka McGuire and "The Sun" by Adriana Reyna, illustrate how two young writers used this form at two of the Family Poetry Days I led in Heppner and Klamath Falls, Oregon, in March and April of 1998.

Cat Moon

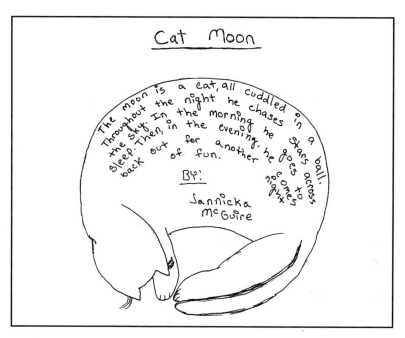

The moon is a cat, all cuddled in a ball. Throughout the night he chases the stars across the sky. In the morning he goes to sleep. Then, in the evening, he comes back out for another night of fun.

BY:

Jannicka
McGuire

The Sun

I am the sun bringing light to the world. My sister is the wind my brother is the sky. The children of Mother Earth all thrive on me to bring them life and joy they need to survive. Each day they come out to play with me. And at the end of the day when peace is on the earth they all dance in the wind and sun.

3. Writing about Nature

Having students observe nature in a classroom or indoor setting and then write poetry or prose about what they sense is an enriching experience. In April of 1998, I attended an Oregon Council for Teachers of English conference in Florence, Oregon. The theme of the conference was "Books on the Beach." After leading a writing workshop on *Writing Across Cultures*, I attended a hands-on seminar that was led by Charles Goodrich, an Oregon author who is currently working as a gardener for the Benton County Courthouse in Corvallis, Oregon.

On a table, he assembled specimens, including a jar of box elder beetles mating on buds of big leaf maple, a conch shell, a sprouting onion, a woodcarving, a loaf of bread, and a tray of water glasses. Participants in the workshop were asked to write about these specimens. For example: "Conch shell/a house built by a mollusk/the colors of dawn..." Lively writing in various genres was the result of this engaging exercise!

I suggested that an additional approach to this exercise with young writers would be to create *acrostic* (spelling) poems such as the following:

O diferous
N arrator of the garden
I ntrospective and intriguing
O h onion, how
N ourishing you are!

I elicited the following group acrostic with a naturalist theme from participants in a Family Poetry Day workshop in Klamath Falls on April 18, 1998:

OUR CITY

K lamath Lake has
L ots of Pelicans and
A lgae
M ountains and Modocs
A griculture
T ule marshes
H ay, sugar beets and potatoes

F lights of eagles
A erie
L ibrary full of fun
L ink River Nature Trail
S ycan marsh

I encourage students to keep a nature journal where they can write about and reflect upon the world around them. Many will want to press wildflowers into the pages of their journal. Others will want to sketch a bird on a branch or the first crocuses peeping up among the gray sidewalks. They may accompany their drawings with haiku. Journals may be artistic, historic, poetic, or scientific in theme and design. These journals may be regarded as miniature time capsules.

In order to foster the naturalist intelligence, it's important to give students the opportunity to explore their senses in natural surroundings. For years, I have had the opportunity to lead summer creative writing workshops through Portland Parks and Recreation in conjunction with the Portland Community Schools. A highlight of the program is our nature trek to the Japanese Gardens. With our nature journals in hand, we pause to reflect, in our own ways, on what we see, smell, hear, touch, feel, and taste.

I asked the students to write haiku and color poems as part of their reflective writing. I tell them about the ancient Japanese character *Ki* (*Qi* in Chinese). *Ki* is a whole-person philosophy that says there should be beauty in the way we live, symmetry between mind and body. The Far Eastern scholars say one should listen to soft music, contemplate flowers and trees, and read poetry and reflect upon it. Beauty relaxes.

I jotted down the following haiku moments in my nature journal as I strolled along the Wildwood Trail in Portland's Hoyt Arboretum. I used the haiku form of writing three short lines celebrating nature and made the poem visual by writing my lines in the shape of a winding path.

SOJOURN

Notice how the violets
seem to share their secrets
among the whispering ferns

As I roam the woodland
with wild trillium
pine self rainbows into fir

A dance of feathers
fills
luminous branches

Lichen
soft as clouds
hold me in their gaze

Frogs
herald
the day

My child heart
   grows
      full

      Never before have I known
    the music of the dark mosses
or the sea within a stone

4. Color Poems

Students will heighten their senses about color and the natural world with this simple yet evocative writing exercise. I have written color poems with students of all ages who enjoy illustrating their thoughts and sharing them aloud.

First, write a color poem together with the whole class. Begin by selecting a color. If the class is studying the sea environment, choose the color sea green, for example. Or, if they are studying constellations, you may wish to choose silver. The possibilities are endless. If you cannot go outside, bring some specimens from the outdoors such as leaves, moss, pine cones, and seashells into the classroom. Create the poem by completing prompts like the ones in the example I have included below. When they are comfortable with the form, students can create their own color poems.

BLUE

   Sounds like...waves
   Smells like...the ocean
   Tastes like...blueberries
   Feels like...a soft petal
   Looks like...the sky

A more subtle approach is to write the color at the top of the page and make the color come to life without writing the prompts, allowing the imagery to speak for itself. For example:

gold is
a crackling fire
autumn leaves
a full moon rising...

The following is a color poem that was written by second-grader Maia Dlugolecki at a Neighborhood Arts Program I led at Sweetbriar Elementary School in Troutdale, Oregon, during the winter of 2000.

MY YELLOW WORLD

Yellow looks like the sun
Tastes like a banana—
Yellow feels warm.
Yellow is Maia in a pretty dress.
Yellow sounds like a bird singing
and smells like a golden delicious apple.

Maia Dlugolecki

CHAPTER TWO

Summer: Blossoming

in the face
of a flower
infinite beauty

Visual/Spatial Intelligence

*No matter how slow the film, Spirit always stands
still long enough for the photographer it has chosen.*
—Minor White

I am awake. I am a camera! This section consists of photographs, poems, and journal entries that have a deep connection to people, places, and feelings. The section is divided into four approaches that facilitate writing activities through the visual domain: photo montage with people, photo montage with place, spirit of place, and inner landscapes. While most of my examples use photographs, you can draw upon any forms of student artwork—including collages, drawings, paintings, and sculptures—that invite students to write.

Natalie Goldberg writes about the connection between writing and the visual arts in *Living Color*. She notes that painting frees her creative flow, which has a profound impact on the way she writes, "When I left painting, I didn't realize that I gave up a deep source of my writing, that place in me where I can let my work flow. When I cut out painting, I cut off that underground stem of mayhem, joy, nonsense, absurdity. Painting was what continually kept those ducts clean and open, because I never took painting seriously. Without painting, sludge gathered at the mouth of the river and eventually clogged any flow."

Over the years, I have experienced the connection between the visual arts and writing in a number of ways. I once visited an African potter who shapes clay in his garage as he retells traditional stories from his homeland. His pottery *is* folklore. Since writing involves the ability to re-visualize and re-create from experience, the visual arts are a natural way to get students interested and involved. For example, when I lead elementary school students through acrostic, alliteration, haiku, and personification writing exercises, I often have them illustrate their poems or turn them into shape-poems. (See the calligramme exercise in the naturalist intelligence section of the first chapter.)

Adding a visual component to writing activities can excite otherwise reluctant students. Tell your students that you are going to review rules of grammar by writing a cinquain poem, and they will frown. If you say instead that they will create cinquain poems as an art activity using newspapers and magazines, your students will, of course, be more excited. Students in grades two and higher will readily immerse themselves in this project when you present it as a hands-on collage activity. (See chapter 4 for cinquain writing.)

1. Photo Montage: Place

Students can explore the intricacies and wisdom of the world around them by capturing images with cameras and combining them to form montages. Have your students make photo montages of the places that are important to them. They can write poems, vignettes, and journal entries to accompany the photographs. Thomas Moore offers insight into the wisdom of nature and place in *The Re-Enchantment of Everyday Life*:

> *All the insight we need could be found in a library, in the great literature of the arts, humanities, and religions, or in meditation on a single flower garden outside the most ordinary house, because nature...is a book too, teaching those who are willing to be its pupils.*
>
> *The world is shouting at us, offering us guidance, but when we're too busy making up our own inadequate answers, we can't hear its voice. There is a sophistication prior to adult learning and modern development of culture, an appreciation for the interiority of nature and the hidden power of persons and places. It's a sophistication that can be lost behind the illusion that our own developed intentions, observations, and values are supreme.*

Field trips provide perfect opportunities to assign the photo montage activity to your students. I have led students of all ages on numerous field trips linked to topics across the curriculum, ranging from Earth Day to Portland bridges, natural history to public art, marine life to the Oregon Trail. I ask students to bring cameras to take pictures of the highlights that emerge throughout the day. I also encourage them to find additional visuals like postcards.

Back at school, students arrange their photo montages

with vignettes, factual information, and comments that relate to the place they have visited. As a class, they may wish to accompany these photo montages with a group poem, as did a group of fourth and fifth grade students at Woodmere Elementary School in Portland, Oregon, who wrote the following acrostic poem about Ft. Clatsop.

THE GREAT ADVENTURE

F is for the trade and freedom.
T is for the trail they took.

C is for caravans and cattle.
L is for the land they traveled.
A is for the animals they hunted and ate.
T is for the tents they put up.
S is for starvation and suffering.
O is for the oxen on the Oregon Trail.
P is for peace the pioneers found in Oregon.

I took the following photo montage while leading a field trip for a group of teenaged Japanese cultural exchange students from Osaka during the summer of 1997. I then researched the origin of this pavilion at the Oregon History Center. The American-Japanese Historic Pavilion, located along the Willamette River in downtown Portland, is a moving tribute to Oregon's first Japanese settlers. The inscriptions on the stones form an evocative montage.

Take a walk around your own city, neighborhood, farm, or seaside. The natural montage of trees, architecture, people, plants, and wildlife make wonderful catalysts for photo montages. The local bookstores, libraries, and museums are good resources for literary and historical information that will complement your montages.

Through the car window

A glimpse of pines.

Oregon mountains.

My heart beats faster,

Returning home.

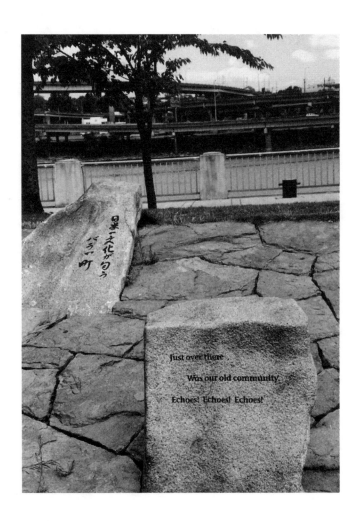

Just over there

Was our old community.

Echoes! Echoes! Echoes!

With new hope,

We build new lives.

Why complain when it rains?

This is what it means to be free.

Glancing up

At red-tinged mountains,

My heart is softened.

A day in deep autumn.

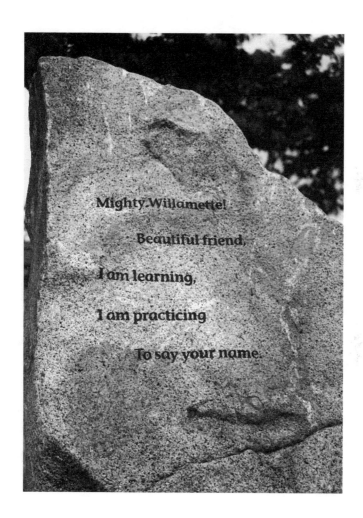

Mighty Willamette!

Beautiful friend,

I am learning,

I am practicing

To say your name.

War and change,
My native land
Once so hard to leave,
Is behind me now
forever.

2. Photo Montage: People

This activity can be used as a prelude to Mother's Day, Grandparents' Day, or some other special family or relationship-oriented occasion. Ask students to close their eyes and think of someone they love. They may draw or sketch a memory about that person or bring in a photograph. The visual aid is meant to evoke memories, and creating the image may deepen the experience. You may wish to link this to a language arts, history, or social studies unit by asking students to create photo montage poems about particular literary or historical figures—characters in a book, for example. Current events are a fine way to make a photo montage from newspapers and magazines. In the following example, I write an elegy to my parents—to my late mother in particular.

MEDITATION ON GRIEF

> Father, I have watched you age.
> Today you are like a boat drifting away.
>
> As I see you ache beside her grave,
> all I can do is ask myself
>
> What will bring you peace?
> Can you endure the majesty of human
>   suffering?
>
> Nothing I can say will cease our grieving.
> Later I will walk—alone—with my own sorrow.
>
> I too shall weep...
> soothed by the sound of waves.

In your dreams you tell me she is still with you
like the vase of cerulean flowers at your
    bedside.

I have a photograph I took of the two of you
    that
I look at now…

Her head rests on your shoulder as it did for
    nearly sixty years.
You're both smiling.

To me, her presence is in the Hoya blossoms
    that
graciously spill their perfume into her silent
    room

a forest of plants that
knew her secrets.

Years ago, when I moved out west for a
    teaching job
I left her my greenhouse.

Today those plants still thrive—green-growing
    leaves
lift their faces to the suns and moons of time.

Mother, thank you for giving me this lucid
    flower
that is my life.

3. Spirit of Place

GREECE

The following poems and photograph were collected from a journal and photo album I kept while living in Greece during the fall of 1985:

THE PHILOSOPHER'S CLUB

After five days of rain,
I'm less of a stranger
in Petros' café—
the only woman here.
I carve a niche
at a corner table.
Here, Greeks talk politics,
soccer, the economy.
An occasional eye turns to my table
but Petros assures them, the Greek
barber and butcher, that I'm
welcome beneath his roof.
My journal is open.
I fill pages with sketches
of men playing cards
drinking coffee
turning their beads
through weathered fingers.
When Petros appears with a tray
of strong coffees
wearing his old slippers
I think here is a man with purpose.

AGORA

    Wreaths of garlic
    baskets of flowers
    hallowed bouquets of
    rosemary, sage—

    Scents of swordfish
    octopus, mullet
    resinous cries of fishermen
    proclaim their catch—

    A trail of blood leads to
    the butcher's stall
    profuse with slaughtered swine
    calm note of a blue canary
    makes me happy to be alive.

    A tiny man sells lottery tickets
    his child pale chrysanthemums

as the man roasting nuts,
sweet almonds, calls
with a different voice:
"Oreha mighala!"
Beautiful almonds!

Pottery, blankets, postcards, aprons
figs, oranges. Olives, eggplant—
"Hela! Hela!"
Move it!
A man pushing his way through the crowd
with a cart full of tomatoes
utters this Zarathustran cry.

Posing Aphrodites throng before the bakery
holding stencil pads and pencils
wearing saffron smiles
before approaching typing school.
Between shopkeepers and neighbors
the spontaneous exchange of *"meras"*
as Eros on his motorbike
honks his love to the world.

ISRAEL

NOTES FROM A JOURNAL

Very first impressions: Ein Carmel ("Eye of the Carmel") is located about twenty kilometers south of Haifa in the heart of the Carmel mountains. If you walk through the cotton fields, you meet a tiny Arab settlement. Donkeys graze in the fields, eucalyptus trees bow in the breeze...a cerulean sea beckons.

Ein Carmel is an agricultural kibbutz. There are

about 450 members who are predominantly Polish.
Three generations of Israelis dwell in small houses.
They speak Yiddish, Hebrew, and French, but very little
English. Volunteers come from all parts of the world:
Belgium, Canada, England, France, Holland, Ireland,
Switzerland. I am the only American here.

* * *

6:00 A.M. to noon, I worked in the banana fields
bagging the bunches before the rains come. This after-
noon I hiked to the Carmel Caves. There, twelve human
skeletons were found that date back to the Early Stone
Age representing the transitional type between Nean-
derthal Man and Homo sapiens. *Nearby, were skel-*
etons of elephants and hippopotami. Also discovered
on this site were a human skeleton and ornamental ob-
jects dating from the Natufian Period (Middle Stone
Age, 8000 B.C.). Scientists have named this Natufian
skeleton "Homo Palestineansis." The caves are situated
among giant cacti. The mouth of the cave where I'm
standing now looks to the west. An aura of timeless-
ness surrounds me as the sun dips into the sea.

* * *

Akko...a subterranean city and fortress still standing
from the time of the crusaders. A city of beauty and de-
cay, successful merchants and poor fishermen. Ascend-
ing the spiral staircase to the old tower, I see TV anten-
nae protruding from the rooftops. The people have
dark, smiling eyes. When you look into them, you see
centuries. You see minutes. You see history.

* * *

Military madness. War on Israel. 1300 tanks to
Golan Heights. Fighting in the Suez Canal. Today we
cleaned the air raid shelters. Preparations for war have

begun. The intensity of this day is one I shall never for-
get. Last night I began the fast for Yom Kippur. I have
not eaten for a day and have forgotten any hunger. By
the light of this candle, I pray for peace. Fathers and
sons leave for the army almost every hour. Wives and
children see them go.

* * *

Yom Kippur: 1973

Tonight I fast for the first time in my life.
All men eighteen to twenty-four years old must go.
Some shake hands.
Shalom.
"Peace."
L'hitraot.
"See you later."
Blackout: 4 a.m. sirens
hours inside shelters
where Polish, Russian, Moroccan women
chant, weep, pray:
Sim Shalom...
"Grant us peace."
At daybreak, I ride the tractor
with the old men to the banana groves.
I help prune trees with a machete.
As Joseph and Isaac murmur
their Yiddish,
low planes fly overhead.
At night, we return by foot
cover the fruits with black plastic
to protect them from oncoming frost.

4. Inner Landscapes

When I travel, I often photograph scenes from cities, forests, arroyos, and shorelines that mirror the way I'm feeling at the time. I call these images "inner landscapes." These texts convey the spirit of the place as well as the landscape of my psyche. In a way, they are like persona poems in that I journey into the photograph and write reflectively; the poems can even be written from the point of view of something in the photograph. To begin inner landscape poems, I think about shooting photographs that reflect the sequence, "I was, I am, I will be." This adds a subtext to the photo journey and to the poems themselves.

OREGON COUNTRY

NEWPORT

I don't know why
the sound of a fog horn
reminds me of places I've never been to.

Often, I'm returned to dreams
of my childhood
the first ocean—

For now, earth and sky hold me
and I continue to climb
the rocky shore.

SEASCAPE

There is no door to enter.
Suddenly you find yourself
a missing person
on a deserted beach
with the tide coming in.
You could stand here forever
with the moon or the sun.
You could stand here
remembering your childhood
among the agate and driftwood
with the far off scent of sea pine
touching the wind.
You could listen to the waters
grow deeper
and deeper—
Will a path
spun by fireflies
to a kind of heaven.

SPIRIT QUEST

Driving through the Gorge,
darkness surrounds
flows all around me.
I remember the way the face
of a thin crescent moon
once answered my own
milkweed stare.
I believed so much then.
Today I long for nothing.
If I could fill my days with waterfalls
I wouldn't be human.
And if radio news isn't bad enough,
the fog and ice seem to have no heart.
I look for some talisman
beyond the dam that drowned Celilo.
Perhaps it's in the voices of larks
that circle Wyeth,
or in the affectionate farmhouse
alone
on a Mosier hillside
by the railroad tracks.
The way the valley opens and turns
anywhere could be another orchard.
In this life I seek voluptuous hours
among boughs and clouds and inlets.
My own wheels abyss
when I feel the rain shake
from the horse's mane
lifting me into a world.

PASTORALE

Evenings
sometimes the cows
call to one another

from farm to farm
sighing like cellos
in all directions

Corn castles
engage in
green dialogue

Wind
folds furrows
copper-pink

Through nodding stalks
of barley grass
crickets hum

And when the goats
chased and fed
lie quiet in their straw

Slowly the stillness
I thrive on
becomes

Musical/Rhythmic Intelligence

Music and nature are gifts, but only if you are willing to receive them.

—Linus Mundy

Musical/rhythmic intelligence can be connected to all areas of the curriculum. In all of the writing activities that I offer in this book, opportunities to enhance writing experiences with music abound. When I offer *Writing Across Cultures* workshops in conjunction with social studies units on African American history, the Holocaust, Native American history, or Japan (to name a few examples), I bring in a library of examples of music. I use blues music by Billie Holiday, Robert Johnson, Lou Rawls, and Bessie Smith to enhance the experience of writing a blues poem. As students write epistles to Holocaust survivors or act out the texts offered in my book, I play Israeli folk music or music of the Holocaust. As students are engaged in the story circle idea offered in chapter 1, I provide Native American flute and drum music to accompany their storytelling. Indeed, the possibilities are endless.

Not all children had the privilege to grow up like I did, among African drummers, Japanese bamboo flautists, classical pianists, cellists, and choral singers. I grew up playing the piano and singing in youth and high school choirs; as a young adult, I played the classical guitar. I bring my appreciation for musical expression to every class I teach. The world of sound is diverse and dynamic.

1. Introduction to Rhythm

As I mentioned earlier in the section on body/kinesthetic intelligence, one way for students to become aware of rhythm is to have them respond to music through movement. Students of all ages enjoy this activity. Adding or creating homemade instruments—such as drums, rattles, spoons, empty boxes, or tambourines—heightens the experience.

1. Put on music with a definite beat (folk, popular, salsa) and have students follow your lead. Take turns appointing leaders and follow the improvisations each individual suggests, whether clapping, drumming, or dancing. With younger children, the teacher can act as leader and lead the rhythm exercise by clapping his or her hands.

2. Sit in a circle with rhythm instruments and accompany the music following the leader who determines the beat. Turn off the music and break into small groups. Create your own rhythms as suggested by each leader and write lyrics. Present to the group.

This activity has been highly successful in arts and communication classes I have taught at the high school level. Students who are meeting their state benchmark standards and students who are musical are eager to share their gifts with those who claim they can't keep a beat. Several of the shyer students, whose strength areas have not yet been tapped, shine. This is a wonderful way to discuss the role of music in many cultures, including our own.

As a supplementary activity, give each student the opportunity to become disc jockey for the day and bring in his or her favorite CD or tape to play during a free time.

2. Listening Walk

Ninety percent of good writing is good listening. Take your students for a listening walk around the block, schoolyard, or neighborhood. Instruct your students to be absolutely silent until they hear a sound, such as a bird singing, a car honking, or the wind; then they can raise their hands. Stop the walk and call on a student who has his or her hand raised. Ask the other students to guess which sound that student heard. Auditory discrimination can be finely tuned among students of all ages by using this activity. I've also led students on a listening walk and asked them to distinguish between soft and hard, quiet and loud sounds as we discuss those dynamics and their relation to the world of words.

3. Writing with Music

I have led journal and poetry writing workshops for people of all ages and walks of life. Writing with music invites students to explore different genres of writing. Students may wish to illustrate their meditations with drawings, watercolors, and photographs.

I am selective, reflective, and goal-based when selecting the music for each particular meditation in this exercise. I must consider my audience first. The following musical suggestions have been highly successful with students I have worked with, from middle school students to Elder hostel members. I am always open to exploring student-suggested musical offerings once we have settled into our workshop routine.

As independent or group writing activities, journeys into

meditation and music can provide inlets into creative expression. The ancient Greek master-teacher Pythagoras believed that different notes of the musical scale correspond to colors of the spectrum. Pythagoras further suggested that the tones of the scale correspond to nine primary currents of energy vibration. This inner mathematical system of music, he suggests, is what invests it with the power to evoke physical, emotional, mental, and intuitive responses.

I don't limit my selection to a particular day of the month if my workshop is one day a week, for example. The important thing is to offer music that matches the theme while exploring the vast world of musical form. Writing a journal response to a ballad, with its particular rhythmic and rhyming verse, is an entirely different experience from writing while listening to Indian raga music, which most often fosters stream of consciousness writing.

Based on Pythagoras's insights, Hal Lingerman offers themes for meditation according to the nine primary tones as shown in the following table:

NUMBER	DAYS OF MONTH	THEMES
1	1, 10, 19, 28:	Focus upon the quickening of the mind—new areas of insight, discovery, research in pioneering territory. (mental focus)
2	2, 11, 20, 29:	Center upon the emotional needs for closeness, partnership, linking, emotional supportiveness, and intimacy; one-on-one relationships and details. (emotional focus)
3	3, 12, 21, 30:	Consider the imagery, the arts, and the self-expression that make life beautiful and romantic. (emotional focus)

4	4, 13, 22, 31:	Concentrate upon planning, form, productivity, regularity, and dependability; do the task well. (physical focus)
5	5, 14, 23:	Enjoy variety, change, physical sensation, travel, contact, and move the body to release energy. (physical focus)
6	6, 15, 24:	Serve the community, group, and family needs; socialize. (emotional focus)
7	7, 16, 25:	Enter the silence and deeper fields of knowledge, research, and meaning. Find out who you are in your divine essence and in your character. (intuitive-thinking focus)
8	8, 17, 26:	Take charge and manage what needs to be done. Find the decisions that must be made; use power and money wisely and benevolently. Use willpower and be successful. (mental-will focus)
9	9, 18, 27:	Live for brotherhood, global unity, and harmony, as all lives work together in the one Life. Practice forgiveness and compassion. Synthesis can lead to transcendence. (intuitive-feeling focus)

Table 1. Nine Theme and Energy Vibrations (from Hal Lingerman's Life Streams, *p. ix.)*

The following suggestions by Lingerman include one example from each theme and are accompanied by several of my own poetic responses.

MARCH 1   OPENINGS

FOCUS:

Instrumental music has a broader spectrum...and it suggests a wider variety...than does the voice. A full orchestra, many types (timbres and colors) of instruments all playing together, offers infinite possibilities for complexities of tension-release; it presents a wide range of emotional tone, intricate rhythms, and varied structures in musical themes, textures, harmony-melody combinations, etc... In the work of a skilled composer, the possibilities for a TOTAL OPENING of the listener's sensibilities are enormous.
— Helen Bonny

MEDITATION:

Today, feel yourself outside, open, clear, perhaps in a beautiful meadow. The air is fresh, the fragrance full, and the flowers beautiful in their colors. You can let the breezes blow through you as you breathe naturally, in and out. In the clear meadow, everything is fresh and open; all staleness can now be released. Feel the openings in the beautiful meadow; the color and music of the meadow allow you openings now.

MUSIC:

I listened to *Tranquility*—instrumentals that harmonize nature with music.

DAYBREAK ALONG THE DESCHUTES

What do the willows know?
Their copper branches
draw me to them.

Here the river rings
with the laughter of otters
illuminating a sacred marsh
where herons rest.

My own heart listens as if tranced
to a wind that holds and
blows through us all.

APRIL 11   HOPE

FOCUS:

And in the night of death, hope sees a star, and listening love hears the rustle of a wing.
— Tennessee Williams

MEDITATION:

In this moment go to your favorite place—a place of peace and hope.

Visualize this place opening to you. It is a place of safety, quiet, and renewal. When you are tired or troubled, you can always come here. Even now, the energies here are helping to give you hope and great peace.

MUSIC:

I listened to *Vision*, the music of Hildegard von Bingen.

HOPE

This is my solace:
a river bathed in first light
ducks clanging their greetings
in gentle jubilation—
Iris open their
blue-flag flowers
hummingbirds succumb
to the prose of nectar.
Afloat on a dulcet cloud,
afloat on a flower,
or dancing on the wing of a swallow—
this is the way it's been with me
since childhood's spidery golden
waiting, watching
the way frost would arrive
on a window
never promised, but always
lacy, intricate
when it did.
Somehow I needed to become lost
before returning—to shore.
Once a stone
now a question
I dream from pools of lapis
making patience my oar.

FOCUS:

> The marvels of God are not brought forth from
>   one's will.
>
> Rather, it is more like a chord, a sound that is
>   played.
>
> The tone does not come out of the chord itself,
>   but
> rather, through the touch of a musician.
>
> I am, of course, the lyre and harp of God's
> kindness.
>
> *—Hildegard of Bingen*

MEDITATION:

What does it mean to be "the lyre and harp of God's kindness"? How can you be like a keyboard waiting to be played? Consider your response to the circumstances that come to you. You can make music today; in the tones that you release, remember that you can be the instrument of divine love and kindness.

MUSIC:

I listened to J.S. Bach's *Goldberg Variations* performed by Glenn Gould.

INNER LANDSCAPE

I started out
this morning
in the fog.

From the road
I watched mist

rise like wood smoke
as I climbed outside
my own shadow.

Now it's late.
Alone in my room
while listening to
Baroque music
a pinch of starlight
cracks me open.

MAY 31   THE COSMIC VIEW

FOCUS:

On the beach at night, alone,
As I watch the bright stars shining,
I think a thought of the clef
of the universe and of the future.
A vast similitude interlocks all,
All distances of space however wide,
All distances of time,
All souls, all living bodies though they be ever
so different,
All nations, all identities that have existed
or may exist,
All lives and deaths, all lives and deaths,
all of the past, present, future,
This vast similitude spans them,
and always has spanned,
And shall forever span them and shall
    completely
enclose them.
                              —Walt Whitman

Look at your present situation in terms of the larger, cosmic view. Feel your place in the great span of lifetimes. Remember the great similitude: All lives are interconnected as they move in the infinite. Find your place in the moment and in the great spaces ahead.

MUSIC:

I listened to *"Satori: Zen Meditation Music for Shakuhachi and Koto"* performed by Riley and Gabriel Lee.

FREEDOM

By starlight, a journey
unfolds of itself
without a road
a pair of shoes
or map.
Blue air
listens between tides.
I lift up my face
to sea shells
chanting messages
shore birds scribble
across the sand.

MAY 23   SONG OF LIFE

FOCUS:

I sing the song of life, with the smile of the sun and the dance of the twilight. I float in the sky to rhythm, with the free spirit and joyous heart.
                                        —*Paramananda*

You can let the song of life flow through you. With a free spirit you can find the rhythm of life's dance. You can break free of limiting habits that are no longer necessary. In the smile of sunshine, find the open road that leads joyously toward discovery and fulfillment.

MUSIC:

I listened to "Dances of John Dowland" performed by Julian Bream.

NEW MOON

I can hardly believe
the vibrant tulips

how green
the hills have become

marsh grasses whisper
moonlit madrigals

again the heart says
yes

NOVEMBER 7   REACH

FOCUS:

The struggle to reach...is itself enough to fulfill the heart of man.
                            —Albert Camus

MEDITATION:

Consider today the ways you are reaching toward a great dream or hope. What goal are you reaching for? What great aspiration do you cherish? Whatever your area of reach, it helps you aim beyond where you are to where you might be. Use your capacity to stretch and to aspire. There is no limit to your reach.

MUSIC:

I listened to Mozart's "Concerto for Flute and Orchestra."

SPRING PALETTE

Today my visitors
are robins
and Mozart

I have a feeling
this music
is making a petal

There's a whole world out there
of spirits
poking their noses

out of earth, seas, sands—
worm, abalone, starfish
become what they are

beautiful
as mysterious
as a drop of dew

aware
of their surroundings
a landscape of dreams

It makes me wonder
in a world that seeks my voice
how do I answer

how does one return
the gift
of being human

FEBRUARY 17   ARIA

FOCUS:

The human voice and music can combine to transform...persons into poets, great lovers, and visionaries... 'It is the best of all trades to make songs, and the second best, to sing them.'
                                    —Alan P. Tory and Hilaire Belloc

MEDITATION:

Aria suggests an air, a melody, or a tune. A melody is accompanied by a single voice that brings deep feelings such as joy, nostalgia, or longing.

MUSIC:

I listened to "Le Mystere des Voix Bulgaire."

"The silver swan, who, living had no note;
when death approached unlocked her silent
    throat."
                                    —Anonymous

ARIA

I fell in love with your hands first.
The way they plucked the strings
of your lute, gracing the silence
with Dowland Ayres and Bach Suites.

I never stopped loving the music
your hands made

until the day
I could no longer trust them.

It was a day in late summer
when cicadas herd the afternoon.
That morning, you would think I would have
felt the harbingers of our autumn

Canada geese and
monarch butterflies
fireweed wearing
pollen trousers.

Though I managed to survive
the verbal abuse of my childhood,
I was still vulnerable
I married you.

You, who were kicked inside-out
as you witnessed your own parents'
marriage fall apart—not to mention
Ted, your bootlegger grandfather

from North Carolina
who beat your grandmother
until she was brain dead—
the only woman you ever loved.

I should have seen it coming
that Thanksgiving your mother
refused to serve me at her table

or that Memorial Day weekend in Yakima
when your father drowned us with gifts:
lawn chairs and kitchen gadgets.

What could lawn chairs mean
in a world where a man and a woman
fold up into themselves
who they truly are?

I became the instrument:
the grandmother your grandfather beat,
the mother you hated,
the son your father smothered with material
    love.
I grew so out of tune with myself
I no longer knew who I was.

That summer afternoon it happened
in our ninth year together
we were walking through the school yard.
The poplars' whispering arms
would soon be turning golden....

I was elated by an invitation
to live and work with the Haida Indians
on the Queen Charlotte Islands.

That's when all the warning signals
translated themselves—

You told me I couldn't go
turned on me and shouted,
"You selfish bitch!" as you
pummeled my belly over and over.

I saw the poplars blur
heard the pitches of children's voices
absorbed in their games
of hopscotch and soccer
ripple and fade

how the sweet smell of blackberries
grew thickly fragrant
as my knees buckled under....

I hold my belly now
as I did then.
From that day on, I couldn't
look you in the eye
and call you my husband.

Days, weeks, months went by.
You gave it to me again and again—
between intervals of intimacy
talk of having children
always when it was least expected.

You didn't want intimacy.
We weren't capable.
You needed a mother first.

Over time, I've learned to move
to my own heart's music.
All but your hands
I've left behind.

I escaped with nothing
but my life.
And the years I've spent
suppressing the scars
have silenced me from others.

I've had to work hard each day
at opening the door.
Today I can walk outside
with my own life in my hands.

Today I can weep into the good wind.
Today I can tell it all
to the other side of the mountain
without looking back.

MARCH 18   UNIVERSALITY

FOCUS:

Great art is universal, for everyone.... Great art and music are for all humanity and forever.... The first element in performance is life and love. Then I think it is important to have much experience and knowledge.
—Carlo Maria Giulini

MEDITATION:

Consider how your sensitivity enlarges.

Watch a pebble dropping into a pond. From the center you can see circles moving out.

Your attention moves from the center outward, expanding to larger circles.

Today your feelings of love can move outward—to one other person, to family and groups, reaching to all humanity, the full family of mankind, and then to all living things.

Expand your reach today; your center reaches in the infinite spaces of limitless universality.

MUSIC:

I listened to Natalie Cole's "Unforgettable."

HARMONY

What we have
is this music

with so many
connecting notes

CHAPTER THREE

Autumn: Harvest

Even fallen leaves
hold the moon
in their palms

Verbal/Linguistic Intelligence

The aspects of verbal/linguistic intelligence are semantics (the meanings of words), syntax (the order among words within a context), phonology (the sounds, rhythm, inflections, and meter of words), and praxis (the different uses of words). These are the dimensions of language from which the poet intuitively works. In his *Frames of Mind,* Howard Gardner describes the poet's extraordinary relation to words, "In the poet...one sees at work with special clarity the core operations of language. A sensitivity to the meaning of words, whereby an individual appreciates the subtle shades of difference between spilling ink 'intentionally,' 'deliberately,' or 'on purpose.' Fascination with language, technical facility with words, rather than the desire to express ideas, are the hallmarks...of a poet."

The purpose of this section is to share several approaches that I have found to be successful for activating verbal/linguistic expression among students of all ages and walks of life. Like the storytelling activities in chapter 1, journal writing also awakens the verbal/linguistic intelligence and is addressed in chapter 4.

1. Found Poetry

This poetry suggestion is one I often use with beginning writers. It is a wonderful way to find topics to write about and to have students discover that poetry is all around us. This suggestion is found in Barbara Drake's *Writing Poetry*:

> *Go to a particular environment—for example, a large department store, a grocery store, or a shopping mall. Walk around. Make a list of sounds or write down things you overhear—conversations, bits of songs, loudspeaker announcements. Work these notes into a poem suggesting the atmosphere of the place or your feelings about the place.*

Natalie Goldberg offers and practices this suggestion in *Writing Down the Bones*. She also encourages us to write in different places—a laundromat or café, at bus stops and airports. A writer who makes use of this technique is Ursula K. Le Guin. The following found poem, from *Buffalo Gals and Other Animal Presences,* illustrates the idea. While Drake's and Goldberg's suggestions work well as independent writing assignments, Le Guin's poem shows us that we can read and reflect upon something as tangible as a newspaper clipping, magazine, or Web article, making the writing of found poems an ideal classroom activity.

FOUND POEM

*However, Bruce Laird, Laguna Beach's chief lifeguard,
doubts that the sea lions could ever replace, or even really aid, his staff. "If you were someone from Ohio, and
you were in the water having trouble and a sea lion approached you, well, it would require a whole lot more
public education," he told the* Orange County Register.
                              —Paul Simon, for AP, 17 December 1984

If I am ever someone from Ohio
in the water having trouble
off a continent's west edge
and am translated to my element
by a sudden warm great animal
with sea-dark fur sleek shining
and the eyes of Shiva,
I hope to sink my troubles like a stone
and all uneducated ride
her inshore shouting with the foam
praises of the freedom to be saved.

2. Letter Poems or Epistles

Writing a letter poem is a wonderful exercise for developing voice. I like this exercise because it offers ways for students to ask questions and explore ideas across the disci-
plines by writing letters to famous authors, scientists, or
historical figures, for example. It also encourages them to
tap into the interpersonal and intrapersonal intelligences in
a way that is similar to Lucia Capacchione's healing work
with the non-dominant hand. (See chapter 4.)

The following is an example of a letter poem written by elementary students at Corbett Grade School in Oregon during an Artists-in-Education poetry workshop that was led by poet-in-residence Tim Barnes in May 1986.

DEAR CARPET,

> I love your outer qualities
> despite your stain.
> Dear carpet, tell me
> what are you like inside?
> You must be strong
> or utterly tolerant.
> If I had feet walking
> on me all day
> I'd go stir crazy.   *—Tracey Chase*

I like to elicit class examples first and discuss the letter writing forms, including salutations. I have students think about asking *who, what, when, where, why,* and *how* questions.

The following is a letter poem written by third-grade students in a writing residency I led at Raleigh Park Elementary School in May 2000 on the twentieth anniversary of the eruption of Mt. St. Helens.

May 18, 2000

Dear Mount St. Helens,

Why do you explode? How do you erupt? When you erupt,
are you mad, or what?

Where does your lava flow? Where does your lava come from?
How hot is your lava?

Who are your Mom and Dad? Do you eat tomato sauce, vinegar, and baking soda?

Why do you have snow on your back? How do you feel inside?

Yours Sincerely,
Mrs. Andrews' third grade class at Raleigh Park Elementary School in Beaverton, Oregon

After students write and share their letter poems aloud, I like to turn this exercise around into a riddle game. Tell students to think of an animal, plant, or season, and write down the answers to the questions that others might ask to find out what they are. For example:

I wear fur.
I hop.
I have long floppy ears.
I like to eat carrots.
What am I?

Elementary school students love inventing these "What am I?" riddles as a secondary activity to writing letter poems. This activity can be used throughout the curriculum. For example, students studying the United States or other countries can write questions to their states and countries and then follow up with the riddle activity. History, science, and math letter poems and riddles may be about historical events, facts, inventors, presidents, or equations.

3. My Father's Dictionary Game

I have always possessed an innate love for words. As a child, I enjoyed exploring sounds, creating secret codes, and enhancing my own vocabulary through a game my father played with all the children. I remember the anticipation I would experience at the end of each week when my father stepped out of his study at dinner time, holding a slip of paper with a new and mysterious word that none of us had ever heard before. These words resonated with meaning and took me on magical journeys—words like *apothecary, mellifluous, meandering,* and *rococo.*

Each week, my brothers, sisters, and I would take turns looking up these new vocabulary words in the gargantuan dictionary beside my father's desk. First, my father would say the word aloud and then spell it. Then, one of us would be selected to look for the definition, write it down, and then use the word in an original sentence. How I adored this game as a child!

These days, I continue to celebrate my love for words with my students. I ask students to find several exotic words in the dictionary that they've never heard before, like *gnu, gouache,* and *xenophobic.* Then they write three definitions, including the correct one and two that they create. The other students take turns guessing the correct definition. The person who guesses the correct definition gets to present his or her new word to the group next. By the end of a class period, our vocabularies have grown with remarkable zest!

For younger students, as well as those for whom English is a second language, I encourage the cultivation of vocabulary gardens. Simply have students bring in pots in which they plant popsicle sticks with labels marked with new words. Each pot may be classified into a particular part of speech. Add invigorating nouns, verbs, adjectives, and adverbs that students come across in their studies each week and have them use these new words in context.

4. Wordplays: Alliterations, Ballads, Limericks

Wordplays foster and enhance verbal/linguistic expression. Alliteration is the deliberate repetition of consonants, vowels, or syllables within a line. Ballads tell a story through narrative and dialogue with a rhythm and rhyme pattern of *abcb*, composed in four-line stanzas. Limerick is a form of light verse from Ireland that has a galloping rhythm in five lines and a rhyming pattern of *aabba*. These are delightful forms of poetry that elementary school students will enjoy. It is helpful to create an in-class example of each of the forms as a model for students to follow.

ALLITERATION

To write alliterations, ask students to choose a letter of the alphabet. Elicit a list of three to seven words that begin with that letter. Take the letter *l*, for example: lion, leaps, lagoon, laughing.

Next, ask students to try to unscramble the words to make a sentence. They may use articles and prepositions that begin with other letters: The laughing lion leaps into the lagoon.

Some students need to brainstorm using a list of words. Others will be able to create alliterations without listing. Students should be encouraged to use the dictionary. Many will want to team up and create an entire alphabet of alliterations!

A   An alien alighted from the algae.
B   Baby baboons balance balls on the balcony.
C   Cats catch catnaps under the camellia bush.
D   Duke the dog ate all the delicious, delightful
    donuts.
E   Everyone envisions an earth alive with
    everlasting evergreens.
F   Fragrant flowers flatter Fiona.
G   Glaciers glare like glass.
H   High in the hills hide huckleberries.
I   I try to imagine islands or igloos in Illinois.
J   Jumping jackrabbits jaunt to the jetty.
K   Kind koalas kayak to Korea.
L   Last one to the lake is a lazybones!
M   Moon monkeys make marvelous magic
    at midnight.
N   Nutmeg night nuzzles the neighborhood.
O   Oceans of oysters offer operatic orations.
P   Passenger pigeons patrol the picturesque path.
Q   Queen Quetzalquietly quilts.
R   Rattlesnakes rattle among red ripe raspberries.
S   Silver stars shine like silky sequins.
T   Tigers trample through the towering tulips.
U   Do you see the UFO underneath the ukulele?
V   Voles on Venus vote.
W   Wind whistles while whale watching the white-
    capped waves.
X   Xenophon wants a xylophone for Xmas.
Y   Yesterday your Yorkshire yelped with yellow jackets.
Z   Zippy zebras zoom to another zodiac to study
    zootomy.

BALLADS

I have found the Web to be an excellent source for providing ballads with musical accompaniment. Students will enjoy learning folk songs from different cultures, from Old English ballads to Bob Dylan, as well as creating their own. I like to bring examples of traditional English, Celtic, and German texts and music to class, as well as folk songs and ballads from world literature collections. We discuss the significance of the oral tradition, eliciting folk songs and sayings from those students who may have recently moved to the United States from another land. Dance forms often accompany these ballads and music. Learning new songs and dances is a way to celebrate and enhance students' awareness of and appreciation for cultural diversity.

Secondary and post-secondary students enjoy researching their roots for ballads, folk songs, proverbs, and sayings that they share with the rest of the class. Discussion fosters verbal/linguistic expression. From troubadours to shamans, the balladeer is in us all.

The following text, taken with permission from Bartleby.com, illustrates the traditional ballad form.

BALLAD: THE WIFE OF USHER'S WELL

THERE lived a wife at Usher's well,
 And a wealthy wife was she;
She had three stout and stalwart sons,
 And sent them o'er the sea.

They hadna been a week from her,
 A week but barely ane,
When a word came to the carline wife
 That her three sons were gane.

They hadna been a week from her
A week but barely three,
When word came to the carline wife
That her sons she'd never see.

'I wish the wind may never cease.
Nor fashes in the flood,
Till my three sons come hame to me,
In earthly flesh and blood!'

It fell about the Martinmas,
When nights are lang and mirk,
The carline wife's three sons came hame,
And their hats were o' the birk.

It neither grew in skye nor ditch,
Nor yet in onysheugh;
But at the gates o' Paradise
That birk grew fair eneugh.

'Blow up the fire, my maidens!
Bring water from the well!
For a' my house shall feast this night,
Since my three sons are well.'

And she has made to them a bed,
She's made it large and wide;
And she's ta'en her mantle her about,
Sat down at the bedside.

Up then crew the red, red cock,
And up and crew the gray;
The eldest to the youngest said.
'Tis time we were away.'

The cock he hadna craw'd but once,
And clapp'd his wings at a',

When the youngest to the eldest said,
  'Brother, we must awa'.

'The cock doth craw, the day doth daw,
  The channerin' worm doth chide;
Gin we be miss'd out o' our place,
  A sair pain we maun bide.'

'Lie still, lie still but a little wee while,
  Lie still but if we may;
Gin my mother should miss us when she wakes,
  She'll go mad ere it be day.'

'Fare ye weel, my mother dear!
  Fareweel to barn and byre!
And fare ye weel, the bonny lass
  That kindles my mother's fire!'

LIMERICKS

Ogden Nash penned the following limerick.

A flea and a fly in a flue
Were imprisoned, so what could they do?
Said the fly, "Let us flee!"
"Let us fly!" said the flea.
So they flew through a flaw in the flue.

Modeling a limerick or two for the class helps the reluctant writers get started and encourages students who are afraid they do not have the ability to rhyme. The following are limericks written by fifth grade students at an Artist-in-Education residency I taught at Corbett Grade School in Oregon in 1991.

SUSHI

There was once a man who liked one dish
because he loved that fish.
It was called sushi
and it was very mushy
but the fish wanted one last wish.

—Geno O'Neil

DEAR, DEAR LORANCE

There
once
was
a horse
named
Lorance
who
tried
to
impress
dear
Florance
He
asked
for
a
dance
but
tripped
on
his
pants
and

that
was
the
end
of
dear
Lorance   *—Brooke Kinney*

5. Spelling Lesson: Anagrams

Word games like *Scrabble* and hangman are great spelling
and vocabulary-building activities. Another way to enhance
verbal/linguistic capabilities is to ask students to make as
many words as they can from each of the words on their
spelling list. A word made by scrambling or transposing the
letters of another word is called an *anagram*.

GROWTH

throw	got	hot
tow	go	hog
two	worth	row

6. Taking a Stand: Announcements, Commercials, Current Events, Debates, Role-Plays

Students become empowered when they play an active role in day-to-day school life. Responsibility, whether it takes the form of being a team captain, cafeteria helper, or patrol girl/boy, fosters an appreciation and awareness of others and builds self-esteem. In addition to these traditional forms, current technology is giving students the opportunity to be seen and heard through video cameras, television broadcasting, and digital photography. I have had the opportunity to lead and observe the following organized school activities that not only develop and increase communication skills, but also prepare students for the real world.

ANNOUNCEMENTS

At Menlo Park Elementary School in Portland, Oregon, each school day begins with the broadcast of announcements read by a pair of students over the PA system. The team reads a prepared bulletin that includes the day's relevant tidbits—such as weather, school news, special events, today's lunch menu—and always concludes with acknowledging students or staff who are celebrating birthdays, a popular saying, or a riddle. Students take turns throughout the year teaming up for this morning ritual. Public speaking improves throughout the school year as students engage in this simple, yet highly constructive and reinforcing activity.

COMMERCIALS

Ask students to make a list of topics that concern them about a particular subject. Take health, for example. The list may include such topics as diet, exercise, hygiene (brushing our teeth and washing our hands), nutrition, and rest. Ask students to cut out pictures in newspapers and magazines that are related to their topics in some way. Ask them to assemble collages. With a timepiece, give each student a minute to present a commercial about their given topic. This activity may be linked across the curriculum. It encourages discussion and participation that may be rehearsed and videotaped for performance.

A way of enhancing self-esteem is to make a commercial about oneself. I have had students in high school and college create collages and present short info blurbs about who they are, their hobbies, and interests as a way to break the ice at the beginning of a new semester.

CURRENT EVENTS

Students may wish to design a weekly newspaper complete with headlines, top stories, and special events. Middle and high school students enjoy organizing committees to establish weekly columns that focus on special interest topics like movies, music, poetry, personal advice, and sports. Have your students become journalists, photographers, and reporters for real-life stories in your community. At many schools where I teach in Oregon, students have designed bimonthly TV broadcasts that summarize school events and are programmed on a regular basis. Another outlet for sharing special projects is via your school district's Web site.

DEBATES

From the historic Lincoln-Douglas debate to the current controversy surrounding genetic engineering, the world around us is rich with topics for debate. Taking a stand on an issue and making a formal presentation is an excellent way to teach to the verbal/linguistic intelligence. Topic analysis, thesis statements, outlining, research, and oral presentation all come into play with this assignment. Give students plenty of preparation time. Form a panel of debaters and judges. With your students, create ground rules for speakers and outline the criteria upon which their speeches will be scored. Switch roles so that each student is a presenter as well as a judge.

ROLE-PLAY

This activity gives students the opportunity to interact with one another through a combination of interpersonal and verbal/linguistic learning. Role-playing may be used in history, language arts, science, and social studies curricula. Students can act out famous historical events, reinvent scenes from stories, or portray moments of scientific discovery such as man's first walk on the moon. You can combine this activity with the creation of murals and posters to engage the visual/spatial intelligence as well.

Role-playing is an excellent way to have students actively participate in real-life learning skills such as building friendships, asking for help with homework, following directions, practicing for a job interview, and understanding illness. I have linked role-playing to a unit on ecology. Students wrote Earth Day poems and acted out being a tree, ocean, river, flower, bird, fish, or frog, then showed what they needed in order to survive.

7. Idioms

Idioms are phrases that have more than one meaning. Collect a list of idioms from your class and create idiom lexicons of popular expressions. Our colloquial language is always changing, and your list will continue to grow. Here are a few idiomatic expressions to help get you started:

> A stitch in time saves nine.
> Cold feet.
> Curiosity killed the cat.
> Happy as a clam.
> It cost me an arm and a leg.
> It's raining cats and dogs.

Logical/Mathematical Intelligence

Logical/mathematical thought processing involves recognizing abstract patterns, using inductive and deductive reasoning, identifying relationships and connections, and using scientific reasoning and problem-solving to perform complex calculations. I teach writing to the logical/mathematical intelligence by providing assignments that emphasize mathematical patterns, such as rhythm and number of syllables, and by asking students to organize their thoughts on paper and create shape poems. The Japanese renga is a poetic form with formal limitations. While a timeline offers an organizational pattern that is linear, clustering (or mindmapping) is a lateral approach to outlining thoughts and observations. The "Calligramme," "Cinquain," and "Imagination Hat" exercises that appear in other chapters are additional forms that bring logical/mathematical processing to life.

1. Renga

Using Korean linked verse as a model, the Japanese developed a more structured form of collaborative writing that uses a strict syllabic pattern. Created by Basho in the seventeenth century, renga is almost like a game, played in all seriousness by its participants.

In *Sarumino* or *Monkey's Raincoat: Linked Poetry of the Basho School*, by Lenore Mayhew, the linking technique of renga is described as follows:

> *One person composes a* hokku, or, *"opening verse," the three lines of this poem containing seventeen syllables distributed in the pattern 5-7-5. This poem must be complete in itself, but the next step is that some other person answers it with a two-line fourteen syllable poem arranged in the pattern 7-7. Then a third person responds to the 7-7 with another 5-7-5, and next a fourth person (or the first poet if only three are writing) responds again with a 7-7. This 5-7-5/7-7/5-7-5/7-7...pattern can be repeated until there are a thousand verses.*

STRUCTURE IN RENGA

A renga goes forward in much the same manner as a conversation does. There is, however, an important difference between renga and a conversational exchange. The renga writer responds only to the lines that directly precede his.

The techniques for linking one verse to another are subtle and various. In Japan, Basho used five words to link verses to one another: *nioi* (scent), *hibiki* (echo), *utsuri* (change or reflection), *kurai* (rank), and *omokage* (mental image). What began in twelfth-century Japan as a poetry contest with highly complex rules has evolved into a form of writing that stresses the links between an idea, feeling, impression, or image in a given verse with the one that precedes it. Contemporary renga writers often choose to establish guidelines for tone, theme, and number of links. These Japanese linked verses flow like a series of word pictures.

RENGA RULES

It is not, however, only the linking techniques that create structure in renga. There are other aids to composition, namely, the renga rules. The renga has no grand plan that strives for sense or ordered thought in the whole; instead, it has a plan similar to that of an abstract painting that strives for a balance of colors or a piece of music that strives for a balance of chords. The renga strives for a balance of images.

The following links from a collection of contemporary renga, *Narrow Road to Renga: Twenty Pilgrims with Jane Reichhold*, illustrate the impressionistic nature of the renga form. These links are from "Lips to a Pond," written by Jane Reichhold and Vincent Tripi:

> tea brewed
> lips
> *vt* to a pond
>
> steam clouds
> *jr* a bird whistle

silence takes over
the mountains take over
vt enough of a dragonfly's wing

the afternoon
jr shapes clear blue

towhees from a bush
feet-shifting
vt red into sky

unfurled
jr the universe collapses

Have students experiment with renga by writing about the seasons. Encourage them to be in the moment and create word pictures as they do when writing haiku. Students enjoy listening to Japanese shakuhachi music while writing these links.

The following is a renga that was written by three junior English students in a class I taught at Nestucca High School in Nestucca, Oregon, during my writing residency (in May 1999) through the Oregon Council for the Humanities' Chautauqua-in-the-Schools program.

AUTUMN

The cycles—dying
Leaves like wings spiraling down
Angels shedding husks

The ground lightens into brown
The angels growing new life

The winged leaves fall
Unto the ground Angel's wings
Brown tinged Angel's wings

A sleep like death we all lie
Awaiting a tomorrow

Until Jack Frost comes
We all wait for a new sun
The sun does now come

Sun in night, it fades away
Light in night, Fall, comes again

2. Timeline

Making timelines is a linear way to present logical/mathematical data across the curriculum. Students will enjoy creating timelines while researching biographies of famous people, monitoring space exploration, or gathering relevant facts about an event in history such as the Civil War.

The creation of a timeline is also a wonderful way for students to outline a personal narrative or autobiography. Ask students to recall the pivotal moments of their lives—both positive and negative—from birth to present. It is helpful to model a timeline as a group by coming up with categories of major life events such as the first day of school, first pet, special memories, travel, new siblings, discovery of a special interest or hobby, etc. Then ask students to record the specific events that have been meaningful to them. Next, distribute materials for students to create their timelines and ask them to accompany these timelines with a personal collage about themselves that may then be shared in a story circle.

Another variation on this idea that is useful for goal-setting is to ask students to draw a timeline beginning with the current date and set down the goals they hope to achieve in five to ten years.

3. Becoming a Number, Shape, Object, Symbol

Linking writing to mathematics is a fun way to explore meanings of words as they relate to mathematical shapes, objects, or symbols. Ask students to close their eyes and imagine that they are numbers, shapes, objects, or symbols. When they begin to write, ask them to take us on a journey as the number 2, the shape of a triangle, a window, or an addition sign (+). Describe yourself. What color are you? Where do you live? Tell us what you see, hear, taste, smell, touch, and feel. Say why you like being what you are. For example: Today I am the number 2. I look like a swan. I live on a mailbox in Manzanita, Oregon. I have a great view. I see juncos at the bird feeder. The scent of fir trees and wood smoke fills the afternoon. The wind howls. Dogs bark. Geese honk loudly before the storm. I can taste the peppermint that grows along the fence. I feel raindrops bounce on my head. I am getting all wet. I like being the number 2 because I have a job to do. I am part of an address.

This activity may also take on the form of a guessing game, in the same way that the letter-writing activity in the verbal/linguistic section of this chapter can. For example: I am shaped like a triangle. I am covered with cheese, tomato sauce, green peppers and mushrooms. What am I?

Students may also wish to become more abstract symbols, such as the mandala, the mandorla, musical notes or notations, or the obelisk. These will make for more complex poems, dialogues, and vignettes and may inspire older students to select a famous mathematician when asked to choose a topic for a biographical research project.

When students become numbers, they can experiment with the layout and line breaks. If you're number one, write a one-word-per-line poem. If you're a multiplication table of three, your word pattern (3, 6, 9, 12...) may increase accordingly.

LACHRYMAE

The
wilderness
looks
around,
departs
through
fog-drift.
Ignorance
mumbles
blind
half-remembering
owl
salmon
river
tree.
A sleep
quiet
as dusk
distances
hearts
into
strangers.
Cormorants
become
unrecognizable
in slick.

Not
one
easy
wave
flows
through
this world.

CHAPTER FOUR

Winter:
Walking in Balance

Intrapersonal Intelligence

The reinvention of our selves occurs through the seasons of knowing. I have found that the following observations, written by Charlotte Joko Beck in *Nothing Special: Living Zen*, offer illuminating ways to think about cultivating self.

> *Wrestling with the reality of our lives is part of the endless preparation of the ground. Sometimes we prepare a little piece of ground well. We may have little insights, moments that spring out. Still, there are acres of land that are not yet prepared—so we keep going, opening up more and more of our life. This is all that really matters. Human life should be like a vow, dedicated to uncovering the meaning of life. It takes the most patient practice to begin to see through that, to discover that the sharp rocks are really jewels.*
>
> *Some ice cubes, because they have only a sporadic practice, change only slightly over a lifetime, becoming*

just a little mushy. Those who truly understand the path and practice diligently, however, turn into a puddle. The funny thing about such puddles is that as other ice cubes walk through them, these ice cubes begin to melt and get a little mushy. Even if we only melt slightly, others around us soften, too....

At intervals we say, "Let me alone. Stay away; just let me be an ice cube." Once we've started to melt at all, however, we can't forget. Eventually what we are as ice cubes is destroyed. But if the ice cube has become a puddle, is it truly destroyed? We could see that it is no longer an ice cube, but its essential self is realized.

As we become softer, we find that to be a puddle attracts a lot of other ice cubes. Sometimes even the puddle would rather be an ice cube. The more like a puddle we become, the more work there is to be done. A puddle acts as a magnet for the ice cubes that want to melt. So as we begin to drip more, we attract more work to ourselves—and that's fine.

I also think of the self as a garden that requires inner nurturing as well as attention and inspiration from others in order to grow and thrive. Several years ago, I wrote the following poem that conveys my aspiration to cultivate my garden.

PLANTING A GARDEN

Today, in a wilderness of calm
I watched a storm surround the countryside.
Trees bowed. Mustard hills disappeared
behind clouds. Soon I was inside
a cat with ears bent listening
as the rain beat wildly against the shingles.

I lit the stove, stared out the window.
The day escaped and I was yet
a stranger to my garden.

These days, my garden is filled with perennials, herbs, and wildflowers. I have trillium, columbine, cosmos, iris, lovage, oleander, shooting star, and lupine. My contract teaching jobs take me to every corner of the state where I continue to melt into the project at hand—whether it be teaching poetry to under-served high school students in the inner city or creating community poetry books with families in rural Oregon. I feel lucky to have so many rich opportunities to feed my garden. I feel grounded wherever I go, and I am always discovering fresh ideas to bring to my students. The following journal and poetry writing suggestions have helped my own writing immensely. These days, my melted puddle gets so big that I feel like a stream!

The exercises offered in this chapter are designed to empower writers to engage in reflective writing as a way to journey towards self-understanding. I begin with two accessible exercises that can be used with students of almost any age, from six to adult, and move to some more complex and introspective forms of journal writing that are designed for use by older students both in and out of the classroom setting. The journal writing prompts have been gathered from experts in the field. Classroom teachers and practitioners will want to be selective in using these prompts. Ground rules should be established to keep journal information private. Specifically designed exercises prompt students, writers, and patients to write from within and explore feelings about love, loss, divorce, illness, and death. The ultimate goal of these exercises is to promote healing and personal growth.

1. Personification/Feelings

From Shelley Tucker's *Painting the Sky* come two innovative writing exercises that I have used successfully with people of many ages, from six to adult. The ease with which these poems unfold is delightful. Writers at all levels can use the following prompts to explore issues that they may have placed on the back burner but are now ready to confront. The first exercise deals with personification. As one school counselor put it, this exercise is like projection. By taking on the persona of a bird or a piano, students can be free to express who they are. This activity lends itself well to use across the curriculum, and the resulting poems can be turned into calligrammes. I often use these prompts in the classroom to explore topics in history, social studies, and conflict resolution. While I suggest that students use the prompts, I encourage them to follow their own voices if they have alternative ways of writing persona (a form of poetry that focuses on "personification") or feelings poems.

A. HONEST POTATOES

Give a Thing a Personality

First, choose an object, a color, or an emotion. Then answer the following questions about it. Be sure to write in complete sentences.

1. What are you?
2. Where do you live?
3. What are your favorite colors?
4. What clothes do you wear?
5. What is your job?
6. Who are your family and friends?

7. Where do you go on vacation?
8. What is your favorite holiday?

EXAMPLE: I am a potato.
I live in the earth and stay warm with a thick, brown blanket.

Start with the words "I am," shown above, or begin sentences with the name of the object.

EXAMPLE: Potatoes live in the earth with their families.
Honest potatoes work in underground banks.

Complete the poem by writing more about your chosen subject. Answering prompts like the ones that follow may help generate ideas.

I AM A MANGO

This morning when I woke up
I was a mango.
I live in Hawaii in an orchard
by the sea.
My favorite colors are the gold of the sun
and the pink of the breeze.
My job is to grow plump and juicy
like my family and friends.
Then, when I am ripe
a little girl will come pick me
and sell me to the tourists.

—*Edna Kovacs*

ONCE IN A PURPLE MOON

I am a purple moon
I live in the sky above
the bats and the owls.
My favorite colors are
the violet of the misty sea
the silver of the ocean
and the brightness of gold
like the sun.
I wear cheese and a night cap.
My job is to make cheese
and guide people in the night.
The sun, clouds, stars, and
all the planets
are my family and friends.
On vacation I go to visit
my best friend, the Sun.
My favorite holiday
is the Fourth of July
because everything is bright.

*—Written by the sixth grade students in Mrs.
Matthews's class at Whitford Middle School in
Beaverton, Oregon, during Young Audiences'
Arts for Learning Week in December 1998.*

B. Love Knows About Friends
Turn a Feeling into a Character

Choose a feeling. Write it at the beginning of each line.
Then complete the following sentences.

_____ is the color of _____

_____ wishes for _____

_____ knows about _____

_____ moves like _____

_____ wears _____

_____ shows us about _____

_____ has a pocket of _____

ANXIETY

Anxiety is no solid color.
It is a blur of reds and blues, greens, grays,
blacks, and yellows
coming together
to form a maze of thoughts and emotions.
Anxiety wishes for an answer,
a purpose,
a meaning.
Anxiety knows about a struggle,
a great war being waged.
Opposing generals send their army in the
maddening fray.
Anxiety moves like the wind,
then stops in an instant
fortifying in the soft ground.
Anxiety wears many masks
and pulls costumes from a dark and dirty closet.
Anxiety shows us a challenge,

a gladiator
to face those who believe they're invincible.
It works from the inside,
tearing at the seams
that hold the framework together.
Anxiety has a pocket full of tricks.

—*By Nathan Miley-Wills, Mt. Tabor Middle
School, May 1998.*

BEING HAPPY

Happiness is the color
of a blue sky
when you get out of school.
Happiness wishes for
poems. Happiness
knows of places.
Happiness moves like
a kitten playing with a
ball of yarn. Happiness
shows us about being
kind to the dog at
the door. Happiness has
a pocket of silver and
gold not like money
but like the love
of a poem.

—*By Laura Hallock, Grade 5, Klamath Falls, Oregon
Family Poetry Workshop, Klamath County Library,
April 18, 1998.*

LOVE

Love is the color of warm colors such as red,
orange and yellow. They make you feel close
and bright like some candle deep down
inside you that has been lit, and you feel like
    not
even the strongest hurricane could blow it out.
Love wishes for another bookend to hold up the
books with you, so the feeling inside the books
doesn't scatter about.
Love wishes for a companion, so it can share its
thoughts and ideas.
Love knows about friendship and how
    important it
is to keep it together.
Love moves like the wind, it can touch you
    softly
or blow you away, but somehow you know you
can appreciate it.
Love wears silk, it's soft across your skin and
you feel comfortable wearing it.
Love shows us about confusion and happiness
and that it's not a toy to be played with.
Love has a pocket full of smiles that never goes
    away.
Love is a precious diamond.

—*By Annika Donaldson, Mt. Tabor Middle School,
May 1998.*

INTIMACY

Intimacy is the color of indigo
the glow in your love's eyes
as you walk together under stars.
Intimacy wears a velvet gown
of trust, hope and faith.
Intimacy is the season of Eternity—
it lasts forever.
Intimacy moves like a swan
graceful and lovely to behold.
Intimacy reminds me of my parents—
married fifty-eight years.
Intimacy wishes for a hand to hold
a heart to live in forever.
Intimacy has a pocket of paradise.
Intimacy knows about love.

—*Edna Kovacs*

2. Cinquain Poetry

Writing cinquain poetry is an excellent way to explore feelings, relationships, and personal growth issues. The following suggestion comes from Arleen McCarty Hynes and Mary Hynes Berry's quintessential chapter, "Facilitating Creative Writing," in *Biblio/Poetry Therapy: The Interactive Process: A Handbook* (North Star Press, St. Cloud, MN: 1994).

This form, invented by American poet Adelaide Crapsey, is related to haiku and tanka. Like them, it depends on brevity and juxtaposition of images. Each line can be described in terms of the number of stresses, syllables, or words it contains. Raymond Luber (1976) has successfully used this mode of writing with both hospitalized and outpatient individuals. This is the format he has adopted:

Content	Length
Line 1: Title—a noun	1 word
Line 2: Describes the title	2 words
Line 3: Action words/phrases about the title	3 words
Line 4: A feeling about the title	4 words
Line 5: Refers to the title	1 word

This example, produced in a bibliotherapy training workshop, illustrates the form. Notice how the configuration of this poem resembles a diamond or a Christmas tree.

Love

strong bond

Sharing, comforting, listening

As necessary as bread

Feeling

The following is a cinquain that was written by students at Kennedy High School in Mt. Angel, Oregon, during an Oregon Council for the Humanities Chautauqua-in-the-Schools workshop I taught in February 2000:

MT. ANGEL:

German village

Hide from rain

Eat sausage at Octoberfest

Quaint.

To expand this exercise, I cut words and phrases from old magazines. Students can use the cut words to create cinquain poems and cinquain collages. They may also want to illustrate their cinquains with original drawings.

FAMILY

Authentic love

Comfort and Joy

Island in the Mist

RE...TING

FREEDOM

Makes Waves

YOU'LL LOVE THE RIDE. YOU'LL LOVE THE SUSPENSION.

WALKING Beyond

The
EVENING STAR

Change

The Ultimate

Did You know

It has the depth of

SNOW

think about it.

ReDesign

THE CHOICE

life more colorful

Can't Live Without It

ConnectioN

(got work to do)

TOUGH ENOUGH TO HANDLE CHILDHOOD.

DISCOVERY IS A JOURNEY

Oh, Grow Up!

LIKE A ROCK

3. Writing Towards Home

I grew up on the south side of Chicago. My childhood was not spent hanging out in the woods or at suburban shopping malls. We did, however, live right across the street from Lake Michigan and Jackson Park. I can remember the many delightful hours I spent playing there with other children my age.

The following poems are childhood memories that were written in response to reading Georgia Heard's *Writing Towards Home*. In the chapter titled "The Full Picture," Heard invites writers to:

> *Return to a moment, a memory, a day in your childhood. Picture it so clearly you can touch it. Divide your paper in half. In the first column, write about this day, this image, in the dewy light of nostalgia—make the sun shine, pretend everything is pleasant. In other words, play it in C major, no flats or sharps. In the second column expand your range. Include any foreboding, fears, shadows, doubts, thoughts that makes this image, this scene, more complex and nuanced than the first version. Read them both. Look at them side by side and compare the two worlds. Which feels more true? Would blending the two describe the truth more accurately?*

BUSTER BROWN

It would be the time of year when thawing snows subside to oozing mud. It would usually come unexpected—like the first lilacs that shock the senses with their vibrant color and scent. It would be Spring…late April, early May… Suddenly the swings would reappear on their chains. There would be

those long, wonderful afternoons in the park playing
hopscotch, Chinese jump rope; endless scavenger
hunts collecting all the round things we could find:
buttons, coins, dandelions. In twos and fours, we'd
all go running to seesaws that creaked and groaned
beneath the weight of our laughter. Ash and oak
found their leaves. Samara pods whirled in spirals.

Buster Buster Buster Brown
What will you give me if I let you down?

I will give you a furry brown bear.
I will give you a doll with curly hair.

I'll give you my mittens
to warm your cold hands.

We shall go to Bremen-Town
and be musicians there.

Buster Buster Buster Brown
What will you give me if I let you down?

To horse-loving Linda
I'll give a palomino.

To Iris, flowers:
dahlias, daisies, wild roses.

To chubby Caroline
an acre of strawberry cheesecake.

To vociferous Vicky
the silence of dusk.

Buster Buster Buster Brown
What will you give me if I let you down?

I will give you a marshmallow tree.
I will give you a ticket to the movies—
all the popcorn you can eat.

I will give you a pocket full of ducats;
a tea party in your honor.
I will give you my hand and my word
and that is enough.

Then, one day, while playing this game,
in a whisper I asked my friend:
Aren't we just dreaming?
My friend smiled back her answer.

We could live beneath a chinaberry tree,
eat honeydew melon, drink peppermint tea.
We could sail away to a distant country
and never have to do any homework.
Sun, you will ripen my fruit.
Moon, you will dazzle me bright.
Wind, let me ride on your back
explore your labyrinthine paths.
Star, I will walk with you at night
for the rest of my life.

MACKINAW ISLAND

When I was seven my parents took
my brother Keith, my sister Stella
and me to Mackinaw Island
We drove from Chicago of a sultry
July morning to a dock in Michigan
I said goodbye to my friends Craig
and Jill in the alley
who promised they'd teach me

how to roll tobacco when I got back
and said hello to a ferryboat ride
across Lake Huron to a tiny island
beneath a mackerel sky
My father told me there'd be
no cars there
just bicycles horses
motorboats and fishing trawlers
which all sounded fascinating
but I didn't believe him
to which he said
I come from Missouri
But when I got to the island
and it wasn't a fable
my brother who was going on thirteen
went to the pool to look for girls
while my sister and I played ping pong
'til we grew bored
and my parents went to a luncheon
where my father gave a speech at the
annual National Macaroni Convention
about the importance of supplementing pasta
with calcium iron vitamins A & D
and when the heads of those pasta companies
caught on to his idea that *hey*! Adding
substance to pasta could be colossal
I wasn't surprised
as I'd heard his wisdom
all my life
And when in the evening
the grownups danced waltzes
and graceful minuets
Keith disappeared and

Stella and I tried our best to behave
but we couldn't help walking up
the down escalator
and down the up
we pestered the bellboy Pete
to crack a smile
and we met the friendliest people
with wonderful names
like Alberto Tartini and Lucia Capello
And in the midst of my childhood
I can remember catching the glow
in my mother's eyes as she whirled
across the ballroom floor
dressed in a turquoise gown
waking the next morning to fog horns
and horses' hooves

In this rites of passage poem, I imagine myself to be a young woman living in South America. For me, experiencing menstruation was like being suddenly transported to another country. I was thirteen years old. I'll always remember my mother's words when I asked her to look at my under garments which I'd hung on the bathroom doorknob just before bedtime. She embraced me that June evening and exclaimed, "You're a young lady now!"

THE GIRL WHO GATHERS OLIVES

1.
I cannot imagine them barren.
One I call father. Another, old friend.
There's another tree with a nest in it
which reminds me of the ladies
who visit for coffee and pastries

smelling like plumeria
mouths like bougainvillea.

2.
Winter days grow humorless—
unconnected with anything
outside the house.
Only the goldfish seem to know.

3.
Now the dazzling lilacs have returned.
I'm aware of slender shoots, capricious
bulbs, willow buds reappearing
and I have outgrown my red and blue cotton
      frocks.

Today I return to grandmother's gate.
Hugging me in her arms,
she calls me her little waif.

I spend the afternoon
reading to her from my books
engaged by her tenderness.

Together we drink *Doce de leite*—
Together we dance
among the pink camellias.

4.
Peeling onions in mid-September,
I prospect mother with the question.

I think I'd rather be a salamander
than wait for the day

she pats the pile of unfinished mending
and says,

"Today you may pick
olives instead."

Into the orchard I'll flutter
filling my basket long into dusk.

Later I'll strew
my first tears of womanhood

into the tiny, porcelain
tea cup.

4. The Integrity Moment
Big Me/Small Me: A Dialogue

Living with integrity is about making a conscious effort to
be your best self even when life is getting the best of you.
People and circumstances can push our buttons. Instead of
reacting rashly and saying or doing things that we may later
regret, we can face our shadows and make conscious deci-
sions about how we deal with others and our own selves.

"Living with integrity centers on intention and choice. Our
life is full of moments when something about who we are,
what we believe in, and how we want our worlds to be are
at stake," says Linda Tobey, Ph.D. In her manuscript of a
book-in-progress, Tobey describes the integrity moment as
being an identity-building practice. According to Tobey, "Integrity is a lifelong process of discovery and creation. During that process, we develop a relationship to ourselves and
what we believe is a good way to live in the world—our own
sense of integrity. Certain moments capture our attention
because something about who we are and what's important
to us is at stake. These moments are *integrity moments*."

We all have moments when we feel in control of our destinies. At other times, we may feel that we have not brought our best selves to the table or that we have given away our power. By being conscious of the differences between our initial impulses and the way we would like to handle a given situation, we can take control of our own actions, which can, in turn, change our self-perceptions.

Tobey attributes the unchecked initial, emotional reactions to what she calls "Small Me." The further considered, self-aware responses to a situation are the product of what she calls "Big Me." Tobey urges us to engage "Small Me" and "Big Me" in a dialogue in order to achieve personal and professional growth. Give all of your feelings uncensored expression in "Small Me" sections. Respond in "Big Me" sections by acknowledging the feelings and suggesting ways that you can deal with them or the situation more constructively. It may help you focus if you think about a specific situation in your life that you wish you were handling differently.

When I asked friend and fellow writer Mary Misel how she would reply to this prompt, this is how she responded:

> Background: 49-year-old woman, 3 husbands, 2 children. 17 years in Portland Shipyards as an electrician, 2 years as a union activist, former Sergeant-at-Arms for the Oregon House of Representatives, now returned to college to complete a psychology degree started in 1972. Intending to go to grad school in the fall if accepted.

Small me: I'm so sick and tired of reading academic writing. Two more terms and it'll be over 'til grad school. I'm sick of studying, trying to get things of little impor-

tance to stick in a brain that is old and full and tired. I've acquired test anxiety. I'm afraid I won't make it. And they're all watching, my friends, my fourth husband, my children. I'm committed, like the time I bungee jumped and had to yell, "5"; then everybody continued the countdown, and I knew I had to jump. Everybody counted down, and I had said, "5."

Big me: Stop whining and buck up. It's two more years; you're not out of the woods yet. Why aren't you studying, you know you're having trouble with statistics. You believe you're a math phobe and then you act on it. You can recognize a self-fulfilling prophecy when you see one; you got an "A" in that class. Healer, heal thyself.

Small me: I'm old and tired and want to get off the merry-go-round.

Big me: You are good with people, you have been places most social workers haven't, and there is a need to fill. This is no waste of time. It will give you peace of mind; I truly believe it.

Small me: Time! That's it, I'm getting older, running out of time. It's downhill from 50. All I want to do is write and garden. It's always a struggle; survival is always tenuous. If only I could win the lottery. Why is it always money?

Big me: Aren't you just guilty because the man in your life is actually supporting you? This is the first one to do that for you; you know you want to stay with this one. You know you're not capable of going to school and working full time. Accept those limits, you are too proud and too stubborn.

Small me: But I'm tired and it's almost spring and I

want to dig in the dirt with the sun shining on me.

Big me: So, that's it, a woman in Oregon in the winter wants the sun. Any other impossibilities? I know you're finally at home with your big hips and menopausal body, but only until you're through the passage.

Small me: I will take care of me when the time comes. I have no idea why this man stays with me; I don't laugh as much as when he met me. I'm about as much fun as a broken arm. I spend most of my time worrying that I may blow it. I'm really scared.

Big me: And that does you a lot of good. Maybe once in a while we could take a break from all this worry. I could use a good laugh, a deep long belly laugh. Don't you think I'm tired too, you're a lot of work to keep up and running. Go weed and pet the cat. Take two aspirins and call me in the morning. I'm on strike tonight.

5. The Power of Your Other Hand
Getting to Know Your Inner Child

Dr. Lucia Capacchione's work with right-hand/left-hand writing taps the potential of the brain's right hemisphere in working with self-help issues. In *The Power of Your Other Hand* (Newcastle Publishing Co., Inc., North Hollywood, CA: 1988) she offers useful exercises that promote self-healing, such as talking to your inner child, helping your body heal, healing your relationships, recovering from addictions, unlocking creativity, and channeling the deep inner wisdom of your true self.

I have found the following exercise to be extremely successful with at-risk teenagers and adults who are interested in the power of healing through journal writing. In a safe and supportive environment, this exercise can be very empowering. If it is too intense for an individual, suggest other dialogue-writing options such as a conversation with your inner teenager, a part of your body, or significant other.

Working with the inner child and nurturing parent is a way of exploring, embracing, recognizing, understanding, and honoring our true selves. As Capacchione notes, we all have a child with playful and creative instincts living within us, a child who needs to be parented. It is up to us to become our own parents and provide the guidance, support, and understanding for our inner children. You can add variety to this technique by dialoguing with the wounded, magical, or playful child.

1. Picture a place that you think would feel comfortable for your inner child, such as the shore of a lake, river, or ocean; a meadow; a garden; or a beautiful room.
2. Now invite your inner child to come into the picture. See this child in your mind's eye. Is it a boy or girl? How old is the child? What does he or she look like?
3. Now start writing a dialogue. Writing with your dominant hand, greet the child, introduce yourself, and ask his or her name. Let your inner child respond by writing with your other hand.
4. Tell the child you want to know about his or her feelings, needs, likes, and dislikes. Then continue the conversation. The nurturing parent writes with the dominant hand, the inner child with the non-

dominant hand.

5. Complete your conversation by asking the inner child for one special thing it wants from you. Work out something that is mutually agreeable, that satisfies the child's needs as well as those of the nurturing parent who is responsible for following through. Make sure you are willing to keep the agreement made to the child. If not, don't make any promises; otherwise you will disappoint the child and cause further hurt.

6. Thank the child for coming out. If you are willing to meet again, agree on a place and time.

DJ Thornley, who practices journal therapy instruction in Washington, wrote the following response to this exercise:

> Here is the letter from me at the age of eleven (written with my non-dominant hand) and then what follows is the letter from me as an adult back to the eleven-year-old. I will then follow it with what I discovered through the process. I did this exercise on May 12, 1998.

Dear DJ,

I am so mad right now! I read a book called White Stallion of Lipizza *by Marguerite Henry. I decided to write a story about the life of the horse in the book. My story was 10 chapters in a small notebook. It took me about 3 weeks to finish it. My teacher saw me writing in class when I was supposed to be doing math. She took it away and threw it in her desk. She said she's going to throw it away later. I snuck in at recess and stole it back. Now I'm banished to the corner. Why can't I just be left alone and why can't she give me back my story before I get home? It's NOT FAIR!*

Love,
Debby

Dear Debby,

There's a lot to learn in school isn't there? I guess I'd be a little upset too if I had spent all that time writing and someone took it away. Maybe your mom could talk to the teacher with you. It's important to respect other people and the rules they have in school. She probably didn't want you to be behind in math and have to take it home to work on. We all know how much you dislike math. I'm sorry you're having such a hard time. Thank you for sharing with me. I gotta go now, but I promise I will write more to you later.

Love,
DJ

This exercise really opened up a can of worms for me. I realized that, as a child, I had never heard someone say, "I'm sorry you are having such a hard time." It was always, "Buck up...keep a stiff upper lip and endure." I felt totally invalidated in my desire to write or to nurture creativity and it was four more years before I began to write for pleasure again. Writing these letters to and from myself gave me validation for those ignored feelings. I was then able to let go of some of the negative messages I had been giving myself about writing all those years.

6. Poetry as Therapy

According to Ken Gorelick, M.D., R.P.T., and Peggy Heller, Ph.D., L.I.C.S.W., R.P.T., co-directors of the Wordsworth Center for Poetry Therapy:

> *Poetry Therapy is older than literacy. Before written language, bards and storytellers wove the beauty of language into individual and collective experience, giving voice to pain and activating the healing process. Eastern cultures have long used poetry to express what is otherwise inexpressible; poetic utterance is most prized. The psalms too reflect this timeless understanding. At the threshold of east and west, the Greeks in their worship of Apollo respected the connection between medicine and poetry. Contemporary Poetry Therapy is conducted by practitioners suitably trained in the discipline of uniting language arts with creative therapeutic techniques. The focus on Poetry Therapy is on the psyche and interrelationships of the participants, facilitator and literature. It is an interactive process whose goal is the understanding and expression of the self. Strategically applied literature is a means to that end, a catalyst. In the diverse settings where Poetry Therapy is practiced, participants responding to published literature feel safer exploring their inner space. By creating their own writings, they name the nameless, crystallize fleeting thoughts, reclaim forgotten memories and complete some of life's unfinished business.*

I had the opportunity to conduct my own poetry therapy through self-directed learning in the twelve-cassette seminar titled *Writing Your Life in Journal & Poem*, which features Peggy Heller, Ken Gorelick, Kay Adams, and John Fox. When

I first listened to the recordings, I was dealing with the process of accepting my boyfriend's diagnosis of B-cell lymphoma. In the poems I wrote after listening to the tapes, I explored the powerful connection between intimacy and illness. The material that continues to spring forth from the journal and poetry writing suggestions in the seminar is raw and revelatory. As I work through the stages of the grieving process, I look at these poems as touchstones towards my own healing. Many of them are inner landscapes, accompanied by photographs.

I have grown tremendously from the ongoing reading, editing, and revising of journal and poetry entries that resulted from the following workshop suggestions.

A. How does writing heal?

This prompt inspired me to write the following poems, which deal directly with the grieving process. Writing has the remarkable power to help individuals heal from addictions, depression, illness, and loss. Numerous studies, such as those pioneered by James Pennebaker at the University of Texas at Austin, reveal that expressive writing can be good for your health. Not only can it act as an excellent source of emotional release, it can also help clarify your life's direction. Since I was twelve, my journal has been one of my best friends.

LYMPHOMA

Talking before bed
and lovemaking,
the black and white
of your disease.
This sadness

swallows me.
Missing pieces
keep me searching
for answers.

My fingers
run through your
full head of hair.
I shape my lips
on your cheek,
across your neck.
Taking you into
my body,
I know how it feels
to be a woman
in the wilderness.

I also wrote the following poem using the metaphor of
sewing to portray the healing process.

LEARNING HOW TO SEW

I think I know
how to gather the threads
of my own sorrow

Slowly I raise
the thimble
to my thumb

aware
of its reassuring
coolness

Little by little
I begin
to mend

the heart
that has been cut
open

While I tangle and untangle
I tell myself
I am learning how to sew

wanting to feel safe
in a land that is
unfamiliar

I give myself permission
to put healing
into my own hands

B. ONE MINUTE FREE-WRITE:
"RIGHT NOW IN THIS MOMENT I..."

Because this journal prompt is a most powerful tool for
self-realization, I would suggest using it at six-month intervals, such as at the fall and spring equinoxes, for example.
Using this prompt at different times to deal with the same
issue in your life is a way of diving deeper into the situation at hand while being gentle with yourself in the process.

I used this technique to deal with love and loss due to a
terminal illness. The following are poems and journal entries
that came out of this prompt at various intervals during my
relationship with Gary. It moves from our discovery of one
another to the realization and acceptance of the inevitable.

When I wrote the following poem in March 1997, we
didn't yet know what Gary's diagnosis or prognosis would
be. I had finally broken through—I know, as I did then, that
I am capable of love, even though our relationship would
be as fragile as glass.

BREAKING THROUGH

We meet again
In the soft deep

wave upon wave
we discover
an inner melody

I have tried to imagine
going back to my island
or you
catching the next train

But I have no desire now
for traveling solo

We have let ourselves know
how it feels to be rain
filling the river
Together we are building
a country with a heart

Believe me when I say
you have made me green
filled me with a radiance
by the light our love has made

Rollo May once wrote: "To love means to open ourselves to the negative as well as the positive—to grief, sorrow, and disappointment as well as to joy, fulfillment, an intensity of consciousness we did not know was possible before." As I continued to work with this journal writing prompt, I experienced the meaning of May's statement in the very core of my being.

I wrote the following poem in June of 1997, after Gary and I experienced a connection between ourselves and the earth while planting pear trees and blueberry bushes on his land.

BLISS

This feels like home—
where a water ouzel
dazzles the afternoon.
Her song spills through
the May Scotch broom
dripping with blossoms and bees.
A tree frog replies
from the deepest pine.
It's good to be alive.
Here, at the meadow's edge
among this wild music
filled with hawk and sky
clouds and cricket prayers—
our embrace becomes a chrysalis.
Sometimes I want to
pencil in rhythms of the world
recreated with you.
I want to memorize the touch
that carries me away like pollen
or the breath that moves
between us
like a lifelong sea.
I speak of love
of the day's honey lit radiance
our hearts tilting sail
somewhere close to Paradise.

Right now in this moment I...

...need to focus on my own healing...my doctoral work. I need to handle this relationship one day at a time. Change is inevitable. I will focus on the good that is coming. I remember reading this by Rumi: "Part of me wants to eat the stones and hold you back when you're leaving."

Later, while looking at a photograph of Gary and me that was taken a year before we learned of his cancer, I asked myself the question again. "Right now in this moment, I...am longing for you." Out came the following haiku.

longing for you
the wick of a candle reminds me
of a wild sea at twilight

Several weeks later, using the same prompt, I wrote this poem of loss.

MISSING YOU

I miss your head on the pillow
next to mine.

I miss the comforting sound
of your breathing.

I miss curling up to your body—
Waking up with you by my side.

I want a field of time with you.
I want what money cannot buy.

Today clouds puff in slowly
across an uncertain sky.

A year or so later, I returned to this prompt again. It was

one of those Indian summer afternoons in Portland, Oregon. I found myself walking by the Willamette River, pausing at a picnic table to write. To my amazement, a great transformation had occurred. I was no longer emotionally hijacked. I was in control of my life. With this newfound inner strength, I returned to my teaching in schools and communities around the state. Through the grief process, I had come to trust and believe in myself. While my inner work would continue, I was aware that I no longer ached. A great healing had taken place.

HERE AND NOW

A barge glides upriver
carrying a load of sawdust.
Black crows call from ashore.
I meditate on the sound the waves make—
the light, sharp and lucid
penetrates the life along the bank—
thistle, sweet pea, silver birch
gray squirrel in white clover
where gulls horde beside a picnic table.
...The barge passes...
The river grows calm.
Along the shore, ducks
dip and dive
in a kind of dance.
I take these moments with me
back to the office.
Talking on the phone, there will be
the glow of early autumn
in my voice.

C. Five-minute free-write: "What's up? What's going on for you right now?"

My journal often depicted the emotional roller-coaster ride that is life with someone who is ill and in denial. I wavered between denial, fear, anger, and acceptance as I tried to deal with Gary's illness.

Today Gary and I were supposed to drive to Seattle to my friend Francine's fiftieth birthday party. As has been the pattern for the past six months, Gary decided to play it by ear until the last minute—not definite about whether he wanted to hang out with his son or go out with 'the guys.' A torrential rainstorm this morning as well as the feeling of being taken for granted by Gary for my endless flexibility and generosity with my time—made me decide to cancel the trip. Instead, I come home to the poetry tapes and journal waiting to receive thoughts without judgment. A journal is a friend that you can count on.

Several weeks later, while listening to an instrumental selection titled "Soul Mates" from *Loon Summer*, the sound of loons and waves moved me to answer the question again. The following poem emerged.

SORROW

No gulls sing
here

Even the mountain
is hidden by clouds

I am a shell
cracking open

I lie exposed on some lonely spot
at the water's edge

unable to weep, unable to forget you
unable to let you go

"Talking to paper is like talking to the divine," Kay Adams
quotes from Burghold O. Holzer's *A Walk Between Heaven
and Earth*. "It is infinitely patient. Silence is a part of the
process," she continues. "The spaces between journal entries speak as eloquently as the words."

D. HEALING STORIES

A story is a place where you can reinvent the truth. Write
a story about your hands and put in something that isn't
true. "Don't be afraid to move into realms that don't his-
torically match the truth but that are emotionally and kines-
thetically relevant to you," suggests Kay Adams.

A HEALING STORY

Some nights I worry about all the insects that
crawl through the grass. Or the place inside the center of trees where the bird song is drawn in. Today I
plant squash—charmed by rivulets of worms—that
churn the soil rich. I gather raspberries. After the
horses cozy into the barn, the wind goes searching
through muslin hay gathering opinions about survival.

E. THE LANGUAGE OF LETTING GO

From Melody Beattie's *The Language of Letting Go* comes
the following reflections to which I responded with poetry:

No one likes a martyr. How do we feel around martyrs? Guilty, angry, trapped, negative, and anxious to get away.

Somehow, many of us have developed the belief that depriving ourselves, not taking care of ourselves, being a victim, and suffering needlessly will give us what we want.

It is our job to notice our abilities, our strengths, and take care of ourselves by acting on them.

It is our job to notice our pain and weariness and appropriately take care of ourselves.

It is our job to notice our deprivation, too, and begin to take steps to give ourselves abundance. It begins inside of us, by changing what we believe we deserve, by giving up our deprivation and treating ourselves the way we deserve to be treated.

Life is hard, but we don't have to make it more difficult by neglecting ourselves. There is no glory in suffering, only suffering. Our pain will not stop when a rescuer comes, but when we take responsibility for ourselves and stop our own pain.

AFFIRMATION: POWER

I'm tired of being crazy with anger
It's time to let go. You've lost me.

We didn't lose anything by loving one another
but I can't ride this roller coaster any longer.
I am not a punching bag or a doormat.
I can't run on empty.
Sometimes I feel like I can't even breathe.
These knots in my stomach
aren't mine. This isn't a relationship.
When I call your name

no one answers.
I am a woman who must stop
sacrificing her self.
I am not a victim.
I am not your mother.
I am not a nurse.
I have been good to you.
I am a strong woman.
I will reclaim my power.
This is a time for healing—
for giving birth to my self.

The following reflection also comes from Melody Beattie's book, *The Language of Letting Go*:

THE GRIEF PROCESS

To let ourselves wholly grieve our losses is how we surrender to the process of life and recovery.

How do we grieve?

Awkwardly. Imperfectly. Usually with a great deal of resistance. Often with anger and attempts to negotiate. Ultimately, by surrendering to the pain. The grief process, says Elisabeth Kubler-Ross, is a five-stage process: denial, anger, bargaining, sadness, and, finally, acceptance. That's how we grieve; that's how we accept; that's how we forgive; that's how we respond to the many changes life throws our way.

Although this five-step process looks tidy on paper, it is not tidy in life. We do not move through it in a compartmentalized manner. We usually flounder through, kicking and screaming, with much back-and-forth movement—until we reach that peaceful state called accep-tance.

When we talk about "unfinished business" from our past, we are usually referring to losses about which we have not completed grieving. We're talking about being stuck somewhere in the grief process. Usually for adult children and codependents, the place where we become stuck is denial. Passing through denial is the first and most dangerous stage of grieving, but it is also the first stage toward acceptance.

We can learn to understand the grief process and how it applies to recovery. Even good changes in recovery can bring loss, and consequently, grief.

We can learn to help ourselves and others by understanding and becoming familiar with this process. We can fully grieve our losses, feel our pain, accept, and forgive, so we can feel joy and love.

In response to this heart-wrenching entry, I did a lot of weeding and weeping in my own grief garden. These two poems depict stages of my own grief process.

ALMOST

> One crust of bread
> before you flew
>
> how the door to my heart
> stayed open

MEDITATION FOR HEART AND WATER

> Waking up in a house of truth,
> it is impossible to hold back the tears.
> I become a raindrop on a stone.
> The rake leans against the house.
> It takes a long time to heal.

Other issues in Beattie's book of meditations that can serve as catalysts for poetry include:

Trusting myself:
Struggling
Accepting chaos
Boundaries
Self-love
Resisting negativity

Commands to the self:
Stop being a victim
Focus on positive energy
Be honest with myself
Transform through grief
Own my own power

Being honest with myself

I wrote the following poem in response to Beattie's book.

CONFESSIONS

In preparation for the treatment
you have cut your hair:
It hurts to see you
looking so pale.

The man I love is dying.

Lying beside me,
you guide my hand
to the lumps on your leg and groin.

Love is pain.

"I'm so lucky to have you," you whisper.

What happened to our harbor?

I press my face against your chest.
My gift of friendship has deepened me
in ways I have never known.

I must trust the darkness.

I fall asleep
listening to
your breathing.

Transforming through grief

I GRIEVE

the loss of a human love.
My raw heart
searches for peace—
healing.
I feel helpless.

You embrace your disease
like a lover.
It is difficult to see you
floating away.
I struggle for clarity.
I suffer.
Again I am alone.

Accepting chaos:

sharp rocks
become diamonds
along the road

Being honest with myself

I am willing
to face
everything.

New beginnings

After the snow falls...

crescent moon
across the lake

the hills
round and smooth

remind me of a dune
I once climbed in a dream

there's a softness
to everything

like pearls
in the night

stars shine
with exuberant clarity

and I think to myself
it is good to be lost

in the beauty
of this world.

Owning my own power

ARIADNE'S THREAD

I need a new season
with leaves changing
the way I'm changing.
The wind's visage
speaks of clarity.
The meaning of migration
comes to me
as I leave my old nest
for new destinations.
Burning in my heart, hope
whispers and waits like a bud
to unfold.
I breathe in the pain of old losses.
Letting go,
I am a woman who feels
maples redden
with the bright punctuation
of crows.
The trees sing with fruit.
It's a ripening time.

Postlude

September 1, 1999; Whistler, BC

Yesterday I left the city behind and said hello to the road. Away from the computer and telephone, I reconnect to the natural world.

Orchid sunrise...peaches in a bowl. At the River of Golden Dreams, I share the dawn with Canada geese. The river sings its lovely song. No one hears the waters grow deeper. Clouds float above mountain peaks. Strolling through a cedar forest, I am filled with the gift of calm.

There's a place I've cultivated inside myself which gracefully accepts the changing seasons. I will continue to water my inner garden. I will continue to befriend my creativity. I recall the glory of discovering my own writing voice and watching it unfold like brushstrokes on some larger canvas that was healing and whole.

I continue to listen and learn, to seek and find fresh ideas for my thinking and writing. While writing this book, I have allowed myself to stretch into the writing exercises as part of my quest for harmony and wholeness through the written word. I am known to be a teacher who keeps her students "up to their eyebrows in writing ideas." My students have, in fact, been my best teachers. It is encouraging to share ideas among kindred spirits. My hope is that this book will nurture, inspire, and free the writer within you.

An Alphabetical Look at Creative Writing Manuals and Sources

KATHLEEN ADAMS' *Journal to the Self: Twenty-Two Paths to Personal Growth* offers specific journaling techniques that help writers achieve greater self-awareness. Written by a master teacher and nationally acclaimed expert in journal therapy, the exercises in this book help individuals work through problems, heal relationships, access the subconscious, interpret dreams, recover from grief, overcome childhood wounds, and much more. For more information about journal therapy training and workshops, contact the Center for Journal Therapy at 1-888-421-2298, or visit their Web site at www.journaltherapy.com.

MELODY BEATTIE's inspirational meditations in *The Language of Letting Go* guide the reader through the recovery process while integrating Beattie's own experiences through daily meditations. Her book is designed to help the reader through the process of recovery and self-care. Dealing with the fundamentals of co-dependency, she emphasizes our need to set healthy boundaries, feel all of our emotions, accept powerlessness, and reclaim our own power.

In my manual, I include several of her meditations that may serve as catalysts for enhancing feelings of self-worth and self-preservation during the grief and healing processes. This book gave me the opportunity to write from within and deal directly with aspects of my personal and professional life. Using Beattie's meditations as prompts, I opened my heart to the healing process and I invite others to do the same.

JULIA CAMERON's *The Artist's Way: A Spiritual Path to Higher Creativity* is a handbook designed for creative people of all walks of life. Cameron's twelve-week program guides the artist through specific exercises that spark creativity while overcoming blocks that inhibit one's full potential. Her book offers ways to link creativity to personal empowerment, fosters new insights, and connects one's creativity with the higher power of the universe. It is a popular workbook suitable for readers who are at least twelve years old. I have used the artist contract at the beginning of the book, in addition to selected exercises, with at-risk adolescents. It is a book to which I will return often for both personal and professional use. While I did not employ Cameron's ideas in my own manual, I believe that the two works would be compatible in an informal workshop or academic setting.

WELLS and CANFIELD's *100 Ways to Improve Self-Concept in the Classroom* is a handbook for teachers and parents. Jack Canfield and Harold Wells have compiled a gold mine of exercises, strategies, and techniques for building and maintaining a positive and supportive environment in the classroom. Success for students is guaranteed through trust walks, creating a personal coat of arms, wishing, and reflective listening exercises, for example. I discovered this book as a graduate student at the University of Illinois in 1976. I used the section titled "Identity, Connectedness, and Power" with Arts and Communication students at Roosevelt High School in Portland, Oregon, who created a multicultural calendar through an ARTSPLAN 2000 + project, as well as with runaway and at-risk girls at the Eastwind Center in Gresham, Oregon, in 1996. Their responses are included in my dissertation. My manual resonates with Wells and Canfield's book, as I am in total accord with teaching toward a humanistic education.

Lucia Capacchione's *The Power of Your Other Hand* guides writers towards using the inner wisdom of the right brain through the use of the non-dominant hand. Using the two hemispheres of the brain allows the inner child to surface. Her exercises offer valuable ways to explore hidden emotions that have been stored away in the unconscious. I have had great success with this technique with at-risk and adult writers who are receptive to self-analysis through journal writing.

In addition, Dr. Capacchione's *Recovery of Your Inner Child* is an instrumental resource for work on the inner child.

Tian Dayton's enlightening book, *The Quiet Voice of the Soul: How to Find Meaning in Ordinary Life*, is a lyrical journey toward love and soul. I read and reflected on the exercises, and the questions posed in the book provided catalysts for poems and journal entries. Dayton's work engages the journal keeper to bond with the self, work on family and significant relationships, make the unconscious conscious, and engage, when necessary, in forgiveness and letting go. Her prompts and passages also deal with healing the wounded self, (re)discovering play, and living with balance and integrity. This meaningful guide is a resource to return to again and again.

BARBARA DRAKE's *Writing Poetry* is a useful textbook that discusses basic features of poetry and offers suggestions for writing. Chapter titles include "The Uses of Memory," "Lists and Catalogs," "Observation and Image, Meditation and Metaphor," "Poems of Address," "Found Poetry," "Found Elements in Poetry and Allusion," "Configurations and Revisions," "Surrealism, Automatic Writing, and Romanticism," "Variations on the Voice: Tone and Persona," "Archetypes, Universal Subjects, and Myth Making," "Games and Experiments," "Form, Forms, Formal and Informal," and "Publishing Alternatives." Examples of poetry make this a successful teaching tool as well as a handbook for individual use. I included the found poetry idea in my manual. Drake uses her book in the creative writing classes she teaches at Linfield College in McMinnville, Oregon. She mentions in the introduction that it is sometimes hard for her to recognize the results of her own assignments. Her emphasis is on the quality of the result, not whether the poem is "right" or "wrong." According to Drake, "the aim is to write an interesting and satisfying poem." I agree with Drake and allow flexibility in the writing suggestions I put forth in my manual.

SHAKTI GAWAIN's fine works include *Creative Visualization*, *Living in the Light: A Guide to Personal and Planetary Transformation*, and *The Path of Transformation: How*

Healing Ourselves Can Change the World. These three extremely valuable guides include exercises, meditations, and affirmations that can enable people to make dynamic changes in their lives and connect with their higher selves. While these texts are not writing handbooks per se, suggested activities may prompt journal writing and poetry. My own practice of keeping a creative visualization notebook has resulted in many of the poems that appear in *Writing with Multiple Intelligences.*

The precepts in *The Path of Transformation* contributed immensely to the way I structured and set out to fulfill the objectives of my book. They include: making a commitment, following inner guidance, finding support, using tools, allowing healing, expressing creativity, and sharing with others.

Living in the Light empowers creativity. In a chapter titled "Becoming a Creative Channel," she writes, "When you willingly follow where your creative energy leads, the higher power can come to you to manifest its creative work. When this happens, you will find yourself flowing with the energy, doing what you really want to do, and feeling the power of the universe moving through you to create or transform everything around you." Your life is your work of art, she affirms in *Creative Visualization.* I turn to Gawain again and again to reinforce my creativity as well as that of my students.

NATALIE GOLDBERG's writing manuals, *Writing Down the Bones* and *Wild Mind,* are user-friendly and enlightening source-books for writers. Both present a Zen-like approach to creative writing. Written in a humorous, free-flowing style, the exercises are a dynamic source for students who want to free the writer within. *Writing Down the Bones* suggests that would-be writers pay attention to details, listen, compose, dream, wander, find poems, and honor each moment. Goldberg offers recipes to writers at all stages of their craft. *Wild Mind* has a gentle "try this" approach. She offers advice about the writer's life, such as the significance of being a reader and cultivating a wild mind as well as the importance of practice. BURGHILD NINA HOLZER describes her book, *A Walk Between Heaven and Earth: A Personal Journal on Writing and the Creative Process*, as a quest. She writes: "I had a goal of sorts. I wanted to produce a book for my students and wanted to document what I had been teaching in class, using the journal as a writing quest. But my particular interest for the journal was the path taken, the walk itself." Thus, this unique guide to journal writing is, in fact, a personal journal. Page after page flows with inspirations and meditations on the creative process. I discovered this text while listening to a lecture on tape offered by Kay Adams in a journal writing workshop from the Poetry Therapy Training Institute's March 1997 seminar (on "Writing Your Life in Journal and Poem"). This book inspired me to make my own manual a unique teaching tool.

EDNA KOVACS' *Writing Across Cultures: A Handbook for Writing Poetry and Lyrical Prose* is a valuable tool for teaching writing to students ages six to adult. In 1993, I received an education-outreach grant from the Metropolitan and Oregon Arts Commissions with a matching grant from Blue Heron Publishing to write and publish this gem. The book was published in March of 1994 and is now in its second printing. From African drum songs to blues, ghazal to haiku, villanelle to the zoo, this playful handbook has dozens of forms to stimulate writers of all ages to write poetry and lyrical prose. Examples and exercises from many cultures (with ethnographies) awaken the creative flow to get writers excited about words. As a teacher and writer, I facilitate the appreciation and awareness of cultural diversity through the written word. I include several of the ideas from this book in *Writing with Multiple Intelligences*, including linked verse and Zen poetry. *Writing Across Cultures* served as a catalyst for *Writing with Multiple Intelligences*.

BARRY LANE's *Writing as a Road to Self-Discovery* helps to shape and sharpen self-expression through specific exercises (see chapter 2 for an explanation of story circles). Lane offers ways for writers to grow both personally and professionally by leading them through the three R's of writing, which are remembering (digging up stories lodged in memory), reframing (questioning and re-seeing the past), and re-experiencing (reliving old stories with new perspectives). For more information on Barry Lane's seminars and works, contact Discover Writing Press, PO Box 264, Shoreham, VT 05770, 800-613-8055, or visit their Web site at www.discoverwriting.com.

DAVID LAZEAR's two workbooks, *Eight Ways of Knowing: Teaching for Multiple Intelligences* and *Seven Ways of Teaching: The Artistry of Teaching with Multiple Intelligences,* translate educational research into practice. Lazear, who specializes in staff development training, brings an understanding of multiple intelligences theory to an audience of all ages. The founder of New

Dimensions of Learning in Illinois, Lazear sums up his philosophy in the following words from the prologue to *Seven Ways of Teaching*: "In a time when programs for the 'gifted' flourish in many schools, I find myself an advocate for the 'giftedness' of every child, if only we as teachers can unlock their full potential."

According to Lazear, teaching intelligence involves four stages. The first stage requires awakening intelligence by activating the senses and turning on the brain. Stage two involves amplifying intelligence by exercising and strengthening awakened capacities. Stage three teaches for and with the intelligences through structured lessons. Stage four transfers intelligence through multiple ways of knowing into the real world.

Seven Ways of Teaching is structured into chapters that correspond to each of the eight intelligences. Each chapter contains practical techniques, lesson plans, and procedures that include discussions that can be a springboard for any lesson across the curriculum. Worksheets, a glossary, and a bibliography conclude this invaluable text.

Eight Ways of Knowing explores each of the intelligences and offers exercises that bring each intelligence to life. I incorporated the idea of "Changing Awareness through Breathing and Walking," which appears in my section on body/kinesthetic intelligence.

JOHN LEE's *Writing from the Body* has helped me overcome writing blocks that were due to negative self-talk, the inner critic, and distractions that robbed me of the ability to concentrate. As Lee notes, "The call to write is a call that's received in the body first. If we are to answer this call, we have to feel every part of our lives. In this book you'll learn the grammar of the gut, the syntax of the sinews, the language of the legs. For everyone who is tired of living life in the little closet between the ears, get ready." Lee's central message is this: In order to write from the truth of our total experience, we must return to our bodies. This refreshing book helped me rediscover breathing meditation and got me on my feet to take refreshing walks, which ultimately became wonderful revision sessions as well as times to empty my mind and just be present in the moment.

HAL LINGERMAN's *Life Streams: Journeys into Meditation and Music* is an inspirational book of daily meditations. Short passages and guided imagery, combined with suggestions for particular pieces of music from New Age, popular, and classical genres, take the reader and listener on a journey to planes of emotional experience. Lingerman has arranged the daily themes for meditation according to Pythagoras's nine primary tones (which are connected by an inner mathematics) that directly correlate to the basic energy flow of the human psyche. Responses may be physical, emotional, mental, or intuitive. For example, a response of "sympathy" would express aspects of a certain vibration called "2" or "twoness," while an emotion of love would describe an aspect of a different energy rhythm called "3" or "threeness."

While Lingerman's book does not ask the reader or listener to respond with a poem or journal entry, I took these meditations to a deeper level by trying out selected meditations and responding to this multi-media experience with poetry. I have also engaged others to do the same in college writing and Elder hostel classes with great success. Someone else may wish to respond to these passages by painting a picture or by improvising movement to the music.

This book offers ways to enter the stillness and quiet the mind, allowing one to connect to the inner self. In addition to supplementing the guided meditations with poetry, I also selected the music in many instances.

ARLEEN MCCARTY HYNES and MARY HYNES-BERRY's *Biblio/ Poetry Therapy: The Interactive Process: A Handbook* is "...The only indispensable textbook for learning the art and practice of bibliotherapy/poetry therapy," writes Kenneth P. Gorelick, M.D., R.P.T., and past president of the National Association for Poetry Therapy. This practical guide for those seeking training in the therapeutic application of literature, including professionals as well as lay practitioners, is comprehensive, impressive, and fascinating. The bibliotherapeutic process, strategies for choosing materials, and the role of the bibliotherapist are all covered thoroughly in this book. The authors include a study guide, practicum suggestions, and further readings to make certification possible using an interactive mentor-supervisor approach. I included the cinquain poetry writing exercise from this handbook in my own manual. In my opinion, this text is essential for anyone who works in the field of poetry.

POETRY THERAPY TRAINING INSTITUTE's twelve-cassette program *Writing Your Life in Journal and Poem* is a recording of a presentation given by Kathleen Adams, John Fox, Kenneth Gorelick, and Peggy Heller in

A Look at Poetry Therapy

Arthur Lerner explains what the term poetry therapy means in his essay "A Look At Poetry Therapy," which appeared in *The Arts in Psychotherapy* in November 1997: "In poetry therapy the accent is on the person. In a poetry workshop the accent is on the poem."

This field, which deals with the creative aspects of one's psyche, has been developing since the 1950s. The poetry therapy profession is a branch of bibliotherapy. Hynes and Hynes-Berry emphasize that "poetry therapy and interactive bibliotherapy are synonymous in most critical respects. Both emphasize the importance between the triad of participant-literature-facilitator as well as the use of creative writing as material."

The first poetry therapy group was established in 1959 by Jack Leedy, a psychiatrist, and his associate, Dr. Samuel Spector. Assisted by Eli Griefer, a pharmacist and lawyer, Leedy directed a clinic at Cumberland Hospital in Brooklyn, New York. In 1970, the Association for Poetry Therapy was instituted, which later became the National Association for Poetry Therapy (NAPT) in 1980. While people were practicing poetry therapy around the country, using sources similar to those used in dynamic psychology, such as Jung and Adler, networking among professionals in the field was still in its infancy.

The *Journal of Poetry Therapy*, first published in 1987, billed itself as "The Journal of Practice, Theory, Research and Education." In 1980 Arleen Hynes developed the National Federation for Biblio/Poetry Therapy (in Minnesota). Then, in 1993, Peggy Heller, Ph.D., R.P.T., a psychotherapist and social worker, Kenneth Gorelick, M.D., R.P.T., a psychiatrist, and Brian O'Neill, M.A., counselor and teacher, established the National Association for Poetry Therapy Foundation in Washington, D.C. The goals of this nonprofit corporation include "promoting education concerning and increasing professional and public awareness in the field of poetry therapy. The Foundation is also interested in fostering educational and research activities in cooperation with NAPT and has as one of its aims the raising of funds for these purposes." Since the arrival of the Internet, the poetry therapy community has continued to flourish on an international level.

Lerner concludes his essay with numerous suggestions for developing the field of poetry therapy. First, he advocates the need for more research, especially of a long-range kind. Research would determine what populations would benefit most from poetry therapy and to what degree. In my opinion, the possibilities for using poetry therapy with people of all ages and backgrounds are endless.

Lerner also believes that special training is needed for therapists who plan to work with specific populations, such as abused individuals, battered women and children, patients with dual diagnoses, family groups, minority groups, the elderly, the homeless population, and those with catastrophic disease (including AIDS). Professional training programs like the Wordsworth

Center for Poetry Therapy currently provide this training.

My interest in poetry therapy was sparked when I met and spoke with Peggy Heller about her work. I had spent over two decades working with exceptional children (from the cream of the crop to the combat zone) in educational, community, and hospital settings. After speaking with Heller, I realized that I was definitely skilled in facilitating poetry-as-healing workshops, focusing on the individual rather than the poem. Intrigued by the possibilities and potential in the field of poetry therapy, I set out to make my contribution through the writing of *Writing with Multiple Intelligences*. Each chapter offers ways for individuals to be engaged in the creative process and enhance their lives by writing from within. As journal therapist Kay Adams

March of 1997 in Washington, D.C. This interactive workshop-on-tape is a source I return to in my teaching and personal writing. It is a rich source for lectures, writing workshops, and discussions that I have drawn from in depth in my chapter on intrapersonal intelligence. While this was a course and not a handbook, I include citation of this program here and have included a look at what poetry therapy is, as the people, teachings, and objectives of this field have made a profound impact on my work.

GABRIELE RICO explores right-brain techniques to release expressive powers through clustering, recurrence, creative tension, and re-vision in her book, *Writing the Natural Way*. Briefly, clustering is a nonlinear brainstorming process that will put you in touch with the subject matter of your writing. Recurrence is a means of discovering a pattern in your cluster that you can use as the basis of a whole story or poem. Creative tension is an exercise in learning to connect opposite images to generate vitality in your style. Revision is a selection process designed to hone and sharpen your work.

I like to use Rico's techniques with young writers who need to get started on a story or poem by putting characters and topics in the center of the circle and then exploring the details of what the writer sees, smells, tastes, touches, hears, and feels. This is also an excellent technique for sharpening details of description and tension in poetry and prose. It is a way I dive deeper below the surface in terms of subtext. It is a non-linear approach to writing that leads to spontaneity and freedom of self-expression.

NATALIE ROGERS explores the connection between the expressive arts and self- and planetary-healing in *The Creative Connection*. Trained as a psychotherapist, she is the founder and co-director of the Person-Centered Expressive Therapy Institute in San Jose, California. Her work facilitates creativity in the expressive arts by making the creative connection through movement, writing, art, music, and meditation.

Rogers trusts in human potential, believes that awareness awakens energy, and offers guidelines and suggestions for achieving self- and global-awareness. As Kahlil Gibran once wrote: "Should you really open your eyes and see / you would behold your image in all images. / And should you open your ears and listen / you would hear your voice in all voices."

Rogers' book is structured in eleven chapters with a bibliography of suggested texts and art materials. The first chapter defines person-centered expressive arts therapy. Chapter 2 discusses conditions that foster creativity in contrast to what blocks it. Chapters 3 and 4 explore specific art, movement, music, and writing exercises. Chapter 5 makes the creative connection between art, music, and meditation. Chapter 6 teaches us how to use the expressive arts with clients. Chapter 7 delves into further applications of the expressive arts. Chapter 8 discovers, integrates, and embraces the Shadow. Chapter 9 engages the reader in the topic of spirituality through the arts, with an emphasis on spiritual imagery practices, such as empathic listening, dialogue practices, being fully present, physical support, and transpersonal aspects. Chapter 10 makes cross-cultural bridges in the expressive arts with Latin America and the former Soviet Union. Chapter 11 considers creativity and consciousness for the future.

Sarumino or *Monkey's Raincoat* explores linked poetry of the Basho School. Translated from the Japanese by Lenore Mayhew, this anthology, which was originally published in 1691, includes four long poems (one for each of the four seasons) written in the linked verse form known as renga. Also included in this book are forty-eight seasonal haiku from the work of Basho and his school. The explanation of renga rules is explored by Mayhew in her introduction. This is an invaluable source book for anyone who wishes to write renga. It is also an elegant anthology of seventeenth-century Japanese linked-verse and haiku poetry. From this anthology, I adapted the linked verse rules this manual.

SHELLEY TUCKER'S *Painting the Sky* offers suggestions for poetry writing that ensure success for writers of all ages. Tucker structures this workbook into units that cover such topics as personification, metaphor, simile, imagery, and alliteration. A glossary and bibliography are also included.

Tucker's approach is to make poetry writing a bridge—a way of enhancing social development and academic success. Her writing suggestions are accompanied by student work, making this a wonderful teaching tool. I have had the opportunity to use this book in numerous community workshops and classrooms in Oregon. Two examples from Tucker's book are included in my manual. I selected them because they provide a guided structure for creating poems that relate to self-concept and personal growth. Tucker also offers guidelines for reading, listening to, and discussing poetry at home and at school. Included in these guidelines are the following axioms that make poetry writing non-threatening by establishing a supportive environment:

Do not criticize your writing.
Do not talk or make noises when someone else is reading aloud.
Do not criticize anyone else's writing.

Fun to read and user-friendly, this vibrant handbook makes poetry writing accessible and enjoyable for anyone who is willing to pick up a pencil.

RIGHTS AND PERMISSIONS

Grateful acknowledgment is made to the following authors and organizations for permission to reprint the copyrighted material listed below.

All students hold the copyrights to their individual poems.

INTRODUCTION

Howard Gardner: For quote from *The Creative Spirit* by Dan Goleman, Paul Kaufman, and Michael Ray. Copyright © 1992 by Alvan H. Perlmutter, Inc. Reprinted by permission of Dutton, a division of Penguin Putnam, Inc., New York, NY.

David Lazear: For multiple intelligences learning styles model. Copyright © 1991 by Skylight Training and Publishing, Inc. Reprinted by permission of Skylight Training and Publishing, Inc., Arlington Heights, IL.

Natalie Rogers: For diagrams and text from *The Creative Connection Process: Expressive Arts as Healing* by Natalie Rogers. Copyright © 1993 by Natalie Rogers. Reprinted by permission of Natalie Rogers, Santa, Rosa, CA.

Jane Hirshfield: For haiku by Izumi Shikibu from *Women in Praise of the Sacred: 43 Centuries of Spiritual Poetry by Women* by Jane Hirshfield. Copyright © 1994 by Jane Hirshfield. Reprinted by permission of HarperCollins Publishers, Inc., New York, NY.

Mihaly Csikszentmihalyi: For excerpts from *Finding Flow: The Psychology of Engagement With Everyday Life* by Mihaly Csikszentmihalyi. Copyright © 1997 by Mihaly Csikszentmihalyi. Reprinted by permission of Mihaly Csikszentmihalyi and Basic Books, Inc., New York, NY.

Edna Kovacs: For "Autumn in the Endless Mountains" by Edna Kovacs. Copyright © 1996 by Edna Kovacs. Reprinted by permission of Edna Kovacs, Portland, OR.

CHAPTER ONE

BODY/KINESTHETIC INTELLIGENCE

Howard Gardner: For quote from *Frames of Mind* by Howard Gardner. Copyright © 1983 by Howard Gardner. Reprinted by permission of Basic Books, New York, NY.

Patricia Lei Anderson Murray: For material from *How to Hula for Body, Mind & Spirit* by Patricia Lei Anderson Murray. Copyright © 1997 by Mutual Publishing, LLC. Reprinted by permission of Mutual Publishing, LLC, Honolulu, HI.

David Lazear: For "Changing Awareness through Breathing and Walking" from *Eight Ways of Knowing: Teaching for Multiple Intelligences*, Second Edition by David Lazear. Copyright © 1991 by IRI/Skylight Training and Publishing, Inc. Reprinted by permission of Skylight Training and Publishing, Inc., Arlington Heights, IL.

John Lee: For excerpts from *Writing from the Body* by John Lee. Copyright © 1992 by John Lee. Reprinted by permission of St. Martin's Press, Inc., New York, NY.

INTERPERSONAL INTELLIGENCE

University of Hawaii Press: For "Linked Verse" by Song Sam-mun, Yi Kae, Shin Suk-chu, Pak P'aeng-nyon, and Yi-sok-hyong from *Anthology of Korean Literature, From Early Times to the Nineteenth Century* compiled and edited by Peter H. Lee. Copyright © 1981 by the University of Hawaii Press. Reprinted by permission of the University of Hawaii Press, Honolulu, HI.

NATURALIST INTELLIGENCE

CHAPTER TWO

VISUAL-SPATIAL INTELLIGENCE

MUSICAL-RHYTHMIC INTELLIGENCE

CHAPTER THREE

VERBAL-LINGUISTIC INTELLIGENCE

AN ALPHABETICAL LOOK AT CREATIVE WRITING MANUALS & SOURCES